JOHNSON

ON

SHAKESPEARE

Oxford University Press, Amen House, London E.C.4

GLASGOW NEW YORK TORONTO MELBOURNE WELLINGTON
BOMBAY CALCUTTA MADRAS KARACHI CAPE TOWN IBADAN

Geoffrey Cumberlege, Publisher to the University

JOHNSON

ON

SHAKESPEARE

ESSAYS AND NOTES SELECTED
AND SET FORTH WITH AN
INTRODUCTION

BY

WALTER RALEIGH

Samuel Johnson

OXFORD UNIVERSITY PRESS
LONDON : GEOFFREY CUMBERLEGE

WGE

*In the impression of 1925 certain corrections were made in the
texts, and a bibliographical note was added on p. 207.*

FIRST PUBLISHED 1908

REPRINTED 1915, 1916, 1917, 1925, 1929, 1931, 1940,
1946 (TWICE), 1949, 1952

PRINTED IN GREAT BRITAIN

CONTENTS

INTRODUCTION

THE history of Johnson's dealings with Shakespeare extends over the greater part of his working life. An edition of Shakespeare was the earliest of his larger literary schemes. In 1745, when he was earning a scanty living by work for the booksellers, he published a pamphlet entitled *Miscellaneous Observations on the Tragedy of Macbeth, with remarks on Sir T. H.'s (Sir Thomas Hanmer's) Edition of Shakespeare*. To this pamphlet, says Boswell, he affixed proposals for a new edition by himself. He had certainly announced these proposals in the advertisements, but no copy of the pamphlet can be found which contains them. It seems likely that after he had advertised his intention, he was discouraged, and changed his mind. When he first thought of editing Shakespeare, he believed that he had only Rowe and Pope and Theobald to contend with and to supersede. Then, while his notes on *Macbeth* were in the press, Hanmer's edition appeared, and it became known to him that the great Warburton was engaged on the same task. Johnson allowed the specimen of his projected edition to go forward, but probably did not print any formal proposals. If any were printed, they are lost.[1] The proposals of 1756 cannot have been written at this earlier date, for in them Johnson speaks, with a certain pride, of his labours on the Dictionary. 'With regard,' he says,

[1] But see p. 207.

' to obsolete or peculiar diction, the editor may perhaps claim some degree of confidence, having had more motives to consider the whole extent of our language than any other man from its first formation.' But the Dictionary was not planned until the scheme for an edition of Shakespeare had broken down. It was necessary for Johnson, if he was to raise himself above the crowd of venal writers, to inscribe his name on some large monument of scholarship. Shakespeare was his first choice; when, perhaps through the timidity of the booksellers, that failed him, he turned his attention to Shakespeare's language, and in 1747 issued the *Plan for a Dictionary*, which he addressed to the Earl of Chesterfield.

The Dictionary was finished in 1755, and Johnson, compelled to find some new means of livelihood, returned to Shakespeare. Warburton's edition had in the meantime been added to the list of his rivals, but his own confidence had increased and his fame was established. The *Proposals for Printing the Dramatick Works of William Shakespeare*, which he issued in 1756, are magnificent in their range and discernment. The whole duty of a Shakespearian commentator and critic is here, for the first time, expounded. The complete collation of the early editions; the tracing of Shakespeare's knowledge to its sources; the elucidation of obscurities by a careful study of the language and customs of Shakespeare's time; the comparison of Shakespeare's work with that of other great poets, ancient and modern—all this and more is promised in the *Proposals*. He seems to have hoped that his edition would be final, and in order to give it that character he promised to reprint all that seemed valuable in the notes of earlier commentators. The whole project breathes that warm air of imagination in which authors design extensive and laborious works. It is possible, but not likely, that he set to work at once on the edition. He originally promised that it should be published in December, 1757. When December came, he mentioned March, 1758, as the date of publication. In March he said that he should publish before summer. On June 27 of the same year Dr. Grainger wrote to Dr. Percy, 'I have several times called on Johnson to pay him part of your subscription. I say, part, because he never thinks of working if he has a couple of guineas in his pocket; but if you notwithstanding order me, the whole shall be given him at once.' Perhaps it was after one of these calls that Johnson, stimulated to unusual effort, wrote to Thomas Warton, on June 1, 1758, 'Have you any more notes on Shakespeare? I shall be glad of them.' Five years later a young bookseller waited on him with a subscription, and modestly asked that the subscriber's name should be inserted in the printed list. 'I shall print no list of subscribers;' said Johnson, with great abruptness: then, more complacently, 'Sir, I have two very cogent reasons for not printing any list of subscribers;—one, that I have lost all the names,—the other, that I have spent all the money.' This magnanimous confession

almost bears out the charge brought against him by
Churchill in his satire, *The Ghost*, published in the
spring of 1762 :—

> He for subscribers baits his hook,
> And takes their cash ; but where's the book ?
> No matter where ; wise fear, we know,
> Forbids the robbing of a foe ;
> But what, to serve our private ends,
> Forbids the cheating of our friends?

There is no evidence that Johnson was in any way
perturbed by Churchill's attack, yet it was the
means of hastening the long-deferred edition. ' His
friends,' says Hawkins, ' more concerned for his reputation than himself seemed to be, contrived to entangle
him by a wager, or some other pecuniary engagement,
to perform his task within a certain time.' In 1764
and 1765, according to Boswell's account, he was so
busily engaged with the edition as to have little leisure
for any other literary exertion. That is to say, he
worked at it intermittently, and satisfied his conscience,
after the manner of authors, by working at nothing
else. In October, 1765, at last appeared *The Plays
of William Shakespeare, in Eight Volumes, with the
Corrections and Illustrations of Various Commentators ;
To which are added Notes by Sam. Johnson*. He had
spent nine years on the work, but a longer delay would
have been amply justified by the Preface alone, which
Adam Smith styled ' the most manly piece of criticism
that was ever published in any country '.

There is nothing singular or strange in this chapter

of literary history. The promises of authors are like the vows of lovers; made in moments of careless rapture, and subject, during the long process of fulfilment, to all kinds of unforeseen dangers, and difficulties. Of these difficulties Johnson has left his own account in the *Life of Pope*. 'Indolence, interruption, business, and pleasure,' he says, 'all take their turns of retardation; and every long work is lengthened by a thousand causes that can, and ten thousand that cannot be recounted. Perhaps no extensive and multifarious performance was ever effected within the term originally fixed in the undertaker's mind. He that runs against time has an antagonist not subject to casualties.' Something steadier and more habitual than the fervour of the projecting imagination is required to carry through a long piece of editorial work. This more constant motive was supplied to Johnson by necessity. He did not pretend to write for pleasure. In a letter to his friend Hector, announcing the new edition of Shakespeare, he says: 'The proposals and receipts may be had from my mother, to whom I beg you to send for as many as you can dispose of, and to remit to her the money which you or your acquaintances shall collect.' In January, 1759, his mother died, and he wrote *Rasselas* in the evenings of one week, to defray the expenses of her funeral, and to pay some little debts which she had left. The famous saying, 'No man but a blockhead ever wrote except for money,' may thus be regarded as the voice of his own hard experience, but it is something more than that. It is Johnson's brief and epigrammatic statement of the unvarying relation between author and publisher. Though it has been cried out against as a wilful paradox, it is the creed of the professional author in all countries and at all times. Young poets may be satisfied with fame, rich amateurs with elegance, missionaries and reformers with influence. But the publisher who should depend for his livelihood on the labours of these three classes would be in a poor way, and indeed, if publishers would communicate to the world an account of their intimate transactions, they could tell how the author who is content with reputation for his first book talks of nothing but money when he comes to proffer his second. He has learnt wisdom. Only vapid sentiment can quarrel with Johnson's view, if his words be taken as he meant them. A publisher of books gains his livelihood by selling to the public that which the public wants, and the man who supplies him with the coveted merchandise, yet scorns to think of the price, is not inaptly described, in the rude vocabulary of colloquial psychology, as a blockhead. The dignity of literature, the high claims of the imagination, the call to advance knowledge and quicken thought—these things also are often regarded by the good publisher. They are still oftener regarded by the good author; they are the motives of his work; and they make of him a bad servant. But why should he talk of these things in the market-

place, where he comes only to ask money for the supply
of that which is sought that it may be sold for money?
The vanity of authors, encouraged by the modesty of
their employers and the superstition of the public, has
imposed a kind of religious jargon on a purely com-
mercial operation. If there are qualities in literature
which are above price, these are also to be found in
the world of manufacture and finance—in that huge
pyramid of loyalty which is modern industry, and that
vast network of fidelity which is modern commerce.
Yet iron-founders and cotton-brokers do not, in dis-
cussing the operations of their profoundly beneficent
trades, express themselves wholly in terms of genius
and virtue.

The later history of Johnson's Shakespeare is soon
told. It was received, says Boswell, ' with high approbation by the publick,' and after passing into a second
edition, was in 1773 republished by George Steevens,
'a gentleman not only deeply skilled in ancient learning,
and of very extensive reading in English literature,
especially the early writers, but at the same time
of acute discernment and elegant taste.' Dr. Birkbeck
Hill throws some doubt on Steevens's claims to taste.
It was Steevens who praised Garrick for producing
Hamlet with alterations, ' rescuing that noble play
from all the rubbish of the fifth act ' ; and who
recommended that the condemned passages should be
presented, as a kind of epilogue, in a farce to be
entitled *The Grave-Diggers ; with the pleasant Humours
of Osric, the Danish Macaroni.* But Steevens deserves

praise for his antiquarian industry and knowledge. To procure him all possible assistance Johnson wrote letters to Dr. Farmer of Emmanuel College and to both the Wartons. He was frequently consulted by Steevens, but the extent of his own contributions is best stated by himself in his letter to Farmer : ' I have done very little to the book.' He never took kindly to the labours of revision ; and his first edition remains the authoritative text of his criticism.

His work on Shakespeare gave Johnson as good an opportunity as he ever enjoyed for exercising what he believed to be his chief literary talent. ' There are two things,' he once said to Sir Joshua Reynolds, ' which I am confident I can do very well : one is an introduction to any literary work, stating what it is to contain, and how it should be executed in the most perfect manner ; the other is a conclusion showing from various causes why the execution has not been equal to what the authour promised to himself and to the publick.' The first of these things he did to admiration in his *Proposals* ; the second he attempts in some parts of his *Preface*. It is plain that he had not been able to do as much as he had hoped by way of restoration and illustration, but it is no less plain that he took pleasure in the accomplished work. Macaulay's statement that ' it would be difficult to name a more slovenly, a more worthless, edition of any great classic ', has nothing but emphasis to commend it. Its author was the inventor of that other tedious paradox, that Johnson's mind was a strange

composite of giant powers and low prejudices.[1] A
wiser man than Macaulay, James Boswell, had already
answered Macaulay's condemnation, which is even
better answered in Johnson's own words : ' I have
endeavoured to perform my task with no slight
solicitude. Not a single passage in the whole work
has appeared to me corrupt, which I have not endeavoured to restore ; or obscure, which I have not
endeavoured to illustrate. In many I have failed
like others ; and from many, after all my efforts, I have
retreated, and confessed the repulse.' Johnson is the
most punctiliously truthful of all English writers, and
from this statement there is no appeal. If his notes
are not so considerable in bulk as those of some of his
fellow critics it is because he had not, like Warburton,
' a rage for saying something when there was nothing
to be said.' It is true that his knowledge of Elizabethan
literature and Elizabethan manners cannot compare
with the knowledge of Theobald before him or of
Malone after him. It is true also that he undertook
no special course of study with a view to his edition.
He had read immensely for the Dictionary, but the
knowledge of the English language which he had
thus acquired was not always serviceable for a different
purpose. In some respects it was even a hindrance.
Johnson's Dictionary was intended primarily to

---

[1] ' Perhaps the lightness of the matter may conduce to the
vehemence of the agency; when the truth to be investigated
is so near to inexistence, as to escape attention, its bulk is to be
enlarged by rage and exclamation.' Johnson, *Preface to Shakespeare.*

furnish a standard of polite usage, suitable for the classic ideals of the new age. He was therefore obliged to forego the use of the lesser Elizabethans, whose authority no one acknowledged, and whose freedom and extravagance were enemies to his purpose. But for all this, and even in the explanation of archaic modes of expression, he can hold his own with the best of his rivals and successors. Most of the really difficult passages in Shakespeare are obscure not from the rarity of the words employed, but from the confused and rapid syntax. Johnson's strong grasp of the main thread of the discourse, his sound sense, and his wide knowledge of humanity, enable him, in a hundred passages, to go straight to Shakespeare's meaning, while the philological and antiquarian commentators kill one another in the dark, or bury all dramatic life under the far-fetched spoils of their learning. A reader of the new Variorum edition of Shakespeare soon falls into the habit, when he meets with an obscure passage, of consulting Johnson's note before the others. Whole pages of complicated dialectic and minute controversy are often rendered useless by the few brief sentences which recall the reader's attention to the main drift, or remind him of some perfectly obvious circumstance.

It must not be forgotten that Johnson was, after all, a master of the English language. He was not an Elizabethan specialist, but his brief account of the principal causes of Shakespeare's obscurities has never been bettered. Some of these obscurities are due to

the surreptitious and careless manner of publication ;
some to the shifting fashions, and experimental licence
of Elizabethan English.   In a few terse sentences
Johnson adds an account of those other obscurities
which belong to the man rather than to the age.
' If Shakespeare has difficulties above other writers,
it is to be imputed to the nature of his work, which
required the use of common colloquial language, and
consequently admitted many phrases allusive, elliptical
and proverbial ; . . . to which might be added the
fullness of idea, which might sometimes load his
words with more sentiment than they could conveniently carry, and that rapidity of imagination which
might hurry him to a second thought before he had
fully explained the first.   But my opinion is, that
very few of his lines were difficult to his audience, and
that he used such expressions as were then common,
though the paucity of contemporary writers makes
them now seem peculiar.'   Let this be compared with
what Coleridge, nearly eighty years later, has to say
on the same question : ' Shakespeare is of no age.
It is idle to endeavour to support his phrases by
quotations from Ben Jonson, Beaumont and Fletcher,
&c.   His language is entirely his own, and the younger
dramatists imitated him. . . . I believe Shakespeare was
not a whit more intelligible in his own day, than he is
now to an educated man, except for a few local allusions
of no consequence.'   In so far as Coleridge seems to
allude to Shakespeare's very characteristic style, his
remarks are true.   In so far as he is speaking of the

wider problem of language, the verdict of modern Shakespearian scholars is wholly on Johnson's side.

These extracts from two great critics are here compared because they show that Johnson's work on Shakespeare has not been superseded. He has been neglected and depreciated ever since the nineteenth century brought in the new aesthetic and philosophical criticism. The twentieth century, it seems likely, will treat him more respectfully. The romantic attitude begins to be fatiguing. The great romantic critics, when they are writing at their best, do succeed in communicating to the reader those thrills of wonder and exaltation which they have felt in contact with Shakespeare's imaginative work. This is not a little thing to do ; but it cannot be done continuously, and it has furnished the work-a-day critic with a vicious model. There is a taint of insincerity about romantic criticism, from which not even the great romantics are free. They are never in danger from the pitfalls that waylay the plodding critic ; but they are always falling upward, as it were, into vacuity. They love to lose themselves in an *O altitudo*. From the most worthless material they will fashion a new hasty altar to the unknown God. When they are inspired by their divinity they say wonderful things ; when the inspiration fails them their language is maintained at the same height, and they say more than they feel. You can never be sure of them.

Those who approach the study of Shakespeare under the sober and vigorous guidance of Johnson will meet with fewer exciting adventures, but they will not see less of the subject. They will hear the greatness of Shakespeare discussed in language so quiet and modest as to sound tame in ears accustomed to hyperbole, but they will not, unless they are very dull or very careless, fall into the error of supposing that Johnson's admiration for Shakespeare was cold or partial. 'This therefore is the praise of Shakespeare, that his drama is the mirrour of life; that he who has mazed his imagination, in following the phantoms which other writers raise up before him, may here be cured of his delirious extasies, by reading human sentiments in human language, by scenes from which a hermit may estimate the transactions of the world, and a confessor predict the progress of the passions.' The great moments of Shakespeare's drama had thrilled and excited Johnson from his boyhood up. When he was nine years old, and was reading *Hamlet* alone in his father's kitchen, the ghost scene made him hurry upstairs to the street door, that he might see people about him, and be saved from the terrors of imagination. Perhaps he remembered this early experience when he wrote, in his notes on *Macbeth*—'He that peruses Shakespeare looks round alarmed, and starts to find himself alone.' In his mature age he could not bear to read the closing scenes of *King Lear* and *Othello*. His notes on some of Shakespeare's minor characters, as, for instance, his delightful little biographical comment on the words '*Exit* Pistol', in *King Henry V*, show with what keenness of zest he followed the incidents of the drama and with what sympathy he estimated the persons. It is difficult to find a meaning for those who assert that Johnson was insensible to what he himself called ' the transcendent and unbounded genius ' of Shakespeare.

His Preface was not altogether pleasing to idolaters of Shakespeare even in his own age. It was virulently attacked, and although he published no reply, his defence of himself is expressed in a letter to Charles Burney ' We must confess the faults of our favourite,' he says, ' to gain credit to our praise of his excellencies. He that claims, either in himself or for another, the honours of perfection, will surely injure the reputation which he designs to assist.' The head and front of Johnson's offending was that he wrote and spoke of Shakespeare as one man may fitly speak of another. He claimed for himself the citizenship of that republic in which Shakespeare is admittedly pre-eminent ; and dared to enumerate Shakespeare's faults. The whole tale of these, as they are catalogued by Johnson, might be ranged under two heads—carelessness, and excess of conceit. It would be foolish to deny these charges : the only possible reply to them is that Shakespeare's faults are never defects ; they belong to superabundant power,—power not putting forth its full resources even in the crisis of events ; or power neglecting the task in hand to amuse itself with irresponsible display. The faults are of a piece with the virtues ; and Johnson as good as admits this when he says that they are ' sufficient to obscure and overwhelm any other merit'. None but Shakespeare, that is to say, could move easily and triumphantly under the weight of Shakespeare's faults. The detailed analysis of the faults is a fine piece of criticism, and has never been seriously challenged.

A deep-lying cause, not very easy to explain, which has interfered with the modern appreciation of Johnson, is to be found in the difference between the criticism of his day and the criticism which is now addressed to a large and ignorant audience. He assumed in his public a fair measure of knowledge and judgement; he ventured to take many things for granted, and to discuss knotty points as a man might discuss them in the society of his friends and equals. He was not always successful in his assumptions, and more than once had to complain of the stupidity which imagined him to deny the truths that he honoured with silence. When he quoted the description of the temple, in Congreve's *Mourning Bride*, as being superior in its kind to anything in Shakespeare, he encountered a storm of protest, the echoes of which persist to this day. His answer to Garrick's objections deserves a wider application: 'Sir, this is not comparing Congreve on the whole with Shakespeare on the whole; but only maintaining that Congreve has one finer passage than any that can be found in Shakespeare. Sir, a man may have no more than ten guineas in the world but he may have those ten guineas in one piece; and so may have a finer piece than a man who has ten thousand pounds : but then he has only one ten-guinea piece. What I mean is, that you can shew me no passage where there is simply a description of material objects, without any intermixture of moral notions, which produces such an effect.' A few days later, in conversation with Boswell, he again talked of the passage in Congreve, and said, ' Shakespeare never has six lines together without a fault. Perhaps you may find seven, but this does not refute my general assertion. If I come to an orchard, and say there's no fruit here, and then comes a poring man, who finds two apples and three pears, and tells me, " Sir, you are mistaken, I have found both apples and pears," I should laugh at him : what would that be to the purpose ? ' Johnson is not attacking Shakespeare ; he is assuming his greatness, and helping to define it by combating popular follies. He knew well that Shakespeare towers above the greatest writers of the correct school. ' Corneille is to Shakespeare,' he once said, ' as a clipped hedge is to a forest.' But he had small patience with the critics who would have everything for their idol, and who claimed for the forest all the symmetry and neatness of the hedge. ' These fellows,' he said, ' know not how to blame, nor how to commend.'

In these and suchlike passages we hear Johnson talking in language suitable enough for a literary club. There is nothing sectarian about his praise ; he speaks as an independent man of letters, and will not consent to be sealed of the tribe of Shakespeare. Modern

criticism is seldom so free and intimate; it has more
the tone of public exposition and laudation; it seeks to
win souls to Shakespeare's poetry, and, for fear of
misunderstanding, avoids the mention of his faults.
It is always willing to suppose that Shakespeare had
good and sufficient reason for what he wrote, and
seldom permits itself the temerity of Johnson, who
points out, for instance, what decency and probability
require in the closing Act of *All's Well that Ends
Well*, and adds: 'Of all this Shakespeare could not
be ignorant, but Shakespeare wanted to conclude his
play.'

It would not be difficult to show that much new
light has been thrown on parts of Shakespeare's work
by the more reverential treatment. Yet perhaps it
has obscured as much as it has elucidated. So fixed
a habit of appreciation is the death of individuality and
taste. Discipleship is a necessary stage in the study
of any great poet; it is not a necessary qualification
of the mature critic. The acclamation of his following
is not so honourable a tribute to a prize-fighter as the
respect of his antagonist. In a certain sense Johnson
was antagonistic to Shakespeare. His own taste in
tragedy may be learned from his note on the scene
between Queen Katherine and her attendants at the
close of Act IV of *Henry VIII* : ' This scene is, above
any other part of Shakespeare's tragedies, and perhaps
above any scene of any other poet, tender and pathétick,
without gods, or furies, or poisons, or precipices,
without the help of romantick circumstances, without

improbable sallies of poetical lamentation, and without any throes of tumultuous misery.' But although this describes the kind of drama that Johnson preferred, he can praise, in words that have become a commonplace of criticism, the wildness of romance in *The Tempest* and *A Midsummer Night's Dream*, and can enumerate and admire the 'touches of judgement and genius' which add horror to the incantation of the witches in *Macbeth*. Like all great critics, he can understand the excellences of opposite kinds. Indeed, in his defence of Shakespeare's neglect of the unities he passes over to the side of the enemy, and almost becomes a romantic.[1]

The history of Shakespeare criticism would be shorter than it is if Johnson's views on the emendation of the text had been more extensively adopted. 'It has been my settled principle,' he says, 'that the reading of the ancient books is probably true, and therefore is not to be disturbed for the sake of elegance, perspicuity, or mere improvements of the sense. . . . As I practised conjecture more, I learned to trust it less ; and after I had printed a few plays, resolved to insert none of my own readings in the text. Upon this caution I now congratulate myself, for every day encreases my doubt of my emendations.' A good

[1] The transformation was completed after his death. I am indebted to Mr. W. P. Ker for pointing out to me that Henri Beyle in his *Racine et Shakespeare* (1822) translates all that Johnson says on the unities, and appropriates it as the manifesto of the young romantics. 'But he told not them that he had taken the honey out of the carcase of the lion.'

part of his work on the text consisted in restoring the original readings in place of the plausible conjectures of Pope and Warburton. Yet he sometimes pays to their readings a respect which he would not challenge for his own, and retains them in the text. He adopts Warburton's famous reading in the speech of Hamlet to Polonius :—' If the sun breed maggots in a dead dog, being a god kissing carrion '—and remarks on it, ' This is a noble emendation, which almost sets the critick on a level with the authour.' Admiration for Warburton's ingenuity caused him to break his own rule, which is sound, and should never be broken. The original reading—' a good kissing carrion '—has a meaning ; and therefore, on Johnson's principle, should stand. Its meaning, moreover, is better suited to Hamlet and to Shakespeare than the elaborate mythological argument implied in Warburton's emendation. If the ' good kissing carrion ' be understood by the common analogy of ' good drinking water' or ' good eating apples ', the grimness of the thought exactly falls in with Hamlet's utter disaffection to humanity. ' Conception is a blessing, but not as your daughter may conceive.' To bring the amended reading into relation with Hamlet's thought Warburton is compelled to write a most elaborate disquisition ; and Johnson might have remembered and applied his own warning : ' I have always suspected that the reading is right, which requires many words to prove it wrong ; and the emendation wrong, that cannot without so much labour appear to be right.'

Johnson's treatment of his predecessors and rivals is uniformly generous; he never attempts to raise his own credit on their mistakes and extravagance. Once, when a lady at Miss Hannah More's house talked of his preface to Shakespeare as superior to Pope's: 'I fear not, Madam,' said he, 'the little fellow has done wonders.' Hanmer he speaks of as 'a man, in my opinion, eminently qualified by nature for such studies'. Warburton was fated to suffer at his hands more than any other commentator, but it is plain from the Preface that he had a grateful remembrance of Warburton's kindness to the early *Observations on Macbeth*. 'He praised me,' Johnson once said, 'at a time when praise was of value to me.' Such praise Johnson never forgot; but he did not allow it to bias his work as a critic. It may be said that he unduly exalts Warburton at the expense of Theobald ('O, Sir, he'd make two-and-fifty Theobalds, cut into slices'), but it was not only personal gratitude which dictated that judgement. Theobald was, without doubt, a better scholar and a better editor than Warburton: there can be no question which of the two has done more for the text of Shakespeare. But Warburton was a man of large general powers, who wrote an easy and engaging style. His long, fantastic, unnecessary notes on Shakespeare are, almost without exception, good reading; which is more than can be said of Theobald's. Johnson's regard for the dignity of letters made him too severe on one who was destitute of the literary graces.

Modern opinion has reinstated Theobald, and is inclined to adopt Foote's, rather than Johnson's, opinion of Warburton. When Foote visited Eton, the boys came round him in the college quadrangle. 'Tell us, Mr. Foote,' said the leader, 'the best thing you ever said.' 'Why,' said Foote, 'I once saw a little blackguard imp of a chimney-sweeper, mounted on a noble steed, prancing and curvetting in all the pride and magnificence of nature,—There, said I, goes Warburton upon Shakespeare.'

Johnson himself would not have been ready to allow any weight to the critical opinions of stage-players. One of his heterodox opinions, says Boswell, was a contempt for tragic acting. In the *Idler* he describes the Indian war-cry, and continues : 'I am of opinion that by a proper mixture of asses, bulls, turkeys, geese, and tragedians a noise might be procured equally horrid with the war-cry.' He was more than once reproached by Boswell for omitting all mention of Garrick in the Preface to Shakespeare, but he was not to be moved. 'Has Garrick not brought Shakespeare into notice?' asked Boswell. 'Sir,' said Johnson, 'to allow that would be to lampoon the age. Many of Shakespeare's plays are the worse for being acted : *Macbeth*, for instance.' This was the belief also of Charles Lamb, who expounded it in his essay *On the Tragedies of Shakespeare*. 'There is somethng in the nature of acting,' he concludes, 'which level, all distinctions. . . . Did not Garrick shine, and was he not ambitious of shining in every drawling tragedy

that his wretched day produced,—the productions of
the Hills and the Murphys and the Browns,—and
shall he have the honour to dwell in our minds for
ever as an inseparable concomitant with Shakespeare?
A kindred mind!' It is a strange kind of heresy that
is the fixed belief of two such critics as Johnson and
Lamb.

But let it be a heresy; one of the chief fascinations
of Johnson's notes on Shakespeare is that they introduce us to not a few of his private heretical opinions,
and record some of his most casual reminiscences.
We are enabled to trace his reading in the *Life of
Sir Thomas More*, and in Sir Walter Raleigh's political
remains, and in the fashionable guide to conversation
translated from the French of Scudery. We learn
some things which Boswell does not tell us; some
even (if a bold thought may be indulged) which
Boswell did not know. We are introduced in the *Life*
to Johnson's cat Hodge, for whom Johnson used to go
out and buy oysters, lest the servants having that
trouble should take a dislike to the poor creature.
But we are not told, what is proved by a note on
Cymbeline, that Johnson passionately protested against
physiological experiments on live animals. Again, is it
not certain that Boswell, if he had known it, would have
told us that his hero wore his boots indifferently, either
on either foot, and further, which is yet a stranger
thing, believed that all other boot-wearers practise
the same impartiality? Boswell can hardly have
known this; yet Johnson's note on the tailor in *King*

John, who, in his haste, falsely thrusts his slippers upon contrary feet, leaves no room for doubt. ' Shakespeare,' says Johnson, ' seems to have confounded a man's shoes with his gloves. He that is frighted or hurried may put his hand into the wrong glove, but either shoe will equally admit either foot. The authour seems to be disturbed by the disorder which he describes.' This is a topic which demands, and would well repay, the expert labours of academic research. Very little is known about Johnson's boots.

A great part of an editor's work is in its nature perishable. Some of his notes are in time superseded ; some are shown to be wrong ; some are accepted and embodied in the common stock of knowledge. Of all Johnson's annotations on Shakespeare those which record his own tastes and habits have preserved most of freshness and interest. It is a privilege to be able to hear him talking without the intervention of Boswell ; we can in some ways come closer to him when that eager presence is removed. It is the greatness of Boswell's achievement that he has made Johnson familiar to us ; but the very zeal and reverence of the biographer inevitably infect the reader, who is admitted to the intimacies of a man of companionable genius as if to a shrine. Boswell made of biography a passionate science ; and viewed his hero in a detached light. Nothing hurt him so much as the implication that any single detail or remark of his recording was inaccurately or carelessly set down. His self-abnegation was complete : where he permits himself to appear it is only that he may exhibit his subject to greater advantage. He invented the experimental method, and applied it to the determination of human character. At great expenditure of time and forethought he brought Johnson into strange company, the better to display his character and behaviour. He plied him with absurd questions, in the hope of receiving valuable answers. All this was not the conduct of a friend, but of a remorseless investigator. And when to this is added Boswell's spirit of humble adoration, it is easy to understand how the whole process has made Johnson clear indeed in every outline, but a little too remote. His eccentricities take up too much of the picture, so that to the vulgar intelligence he has always seemed something of a monster. Even those who love Johnson fall too easily into Boswell's attitude, and observe, and listen, and wonder. It is good to remember that the dictator, when he was in a happy vein, was, above most men, sensible, courteous and friendly. The best of his notes on Shakespeare, like the best of his spoken remarks, invite discussion and quicken thought. What a conversation might have been started at the club by his brief observation on Gaunt's speech in *Richard II* :

Shorten my days thou canst with sullen sorrow,
And pluck nights from me, but not lend a morrow.

' It is matter of very melancholy consideration,' says Johnson, ' that all human advantages confer more power of doing evil than good.' No doubt the reflection is highly characteristic of its author, but we are too much accustomed to let our interest in the character overshadow our interest in the truth. Johnson's talk was free from self-consciousness; but Boswell, when he was in the room, was conscious of one person only, so that a kind of self-consciousness by proxy is the impression conveyed. There is no greater enemy to the freedom and delight of social intercourse than the man who is always going back on what has just been said, to praise its cleverness, to guess its motive, or to show how it illustrates the character of the speaker. Boswell was not, of course, guilty of this particular kind of ill-breeding; but the very necessities of his record produce something of a like effect. The reader who desires to have Johnson to himself for an hour, with no interpreter, cannot do better than turn to the notes on Shakespeare. They are written informally and fluently; they are packed full of observation and wisdom; and their only fault is that they are all too few.

WALTER RALEIGH.

OXFORD
May, 1908.

PROLOGUE

SPOKEN by MR. GARRICK,

At the Opening of the THEATRE-ROYAL,
DRURY-LANE, 1747.

WHEN Learning's triumph o'er her barbarous foes
First rear'd the stage, immortal *Shakespeare* rose;
Each change of many-colour'd life he drew,
Exhausted worlds, and then imagin'd new:
Existence saw him spurn her bounded reign,
And panting time toil d after him in vain.
His powerful strokes presiding truth impress'd,
And unresisted passion storm'd the breast.

PROPOSALS FOR PRINTING THE

DRAMATICK WORKS OF

WILLIAM SHAKESPEARE

(1756)

WHEN the works of *Shakespeare* are, after so many editions, again offered to the Publick, it will doubtless be inquired, why *Shakespeare* stands in more need of critical assistance than any other of the *English* writers, and what are the deficiencies of the late attempts, which another editor may hope to supply?

The business of him that republishes an ancient book is, to correct what is corrupt, and to explain what is obscure. To have a text corrupt in many places, and in many doubtful, is, among the authors that have written since the use of types, almost peculiar to *Shakespeare*. Most writers, by publishing their own works, prevent all various readings, and preclude all conjectural criticism. Books indeed are sometimes published after the death of him who produced them; but they are better secured from corruption than these unfortunate compositions. They subsist in a single copy, written or revised by the author; and the faults of the printed volume can be only faults of one descent.

But of the works of *Shakespeare* the condition has been far different: he sold them, not to be printed, but to be played. They were immediately copied for the actors, and multiplied by transcript after transcript, vitiated by the blunders of the penman, or changed by the affectation of the player; perhaps enlarged to introduce a jest, or mutilated to shorten the representation; and printed at last without the concurrence of the author, without the consent of the proprietor, from compilations made by chance or by stealth out of the separate parts written for the theatre: and thus thrust into the world surreptitiously and hastily, they suffered another depravation from the ignorance and negligence of the printers, as every man who knows the state of the press in that age will readily conceive.

It is not easy for invention to bring together so many causes concurring to vitiate a text. No other author ever gave up his works to fortune and time with so little care: no books could be left in hands so likely to injure them, as plays frequently acted, yet continued in manuscript: no other transcribers were likely to be so little qualified for their task as those who copied for the stage, at a time when the lower ranks of the people were universally illiterate: no other editions were made from fragments so minutely broken, and so fortuitously reunited; and in no other age was the art of printing in such unskilful hands.

With the causes of corruption that make the revisal of *Shakespeare*'s dramatick pieces necessary, may be enumerated the causes of obscurity, which may be partly imputed to his age, and partly to himself.

When a writer outlives his contemporaries, and remains almost the only unforgotten name of a distant time, he is necessarily obscure. Every age has its modes of speech, and its cast of thought; which, though easily explained when there are many books to be compared with each other, become sometimes unintelligible and always difficult, when there are no parallel passages that may conduce to their illustration. *Shakespeare* is the first considerable author of sublime or familiar dialogue in our language. Of the books which he read, and from which he formed his style, some perhaps have perished, and the rest are neglected. His imitations are therefore unnoted, his allusions are undiscovered, and many beauties, both of pleasantry and greatness, are lost with the objects to which they were united, as the figures vanish when the canvass has decayed.

It is the great excellence of *Shakespeare*, that he drew his scenes from nature, and from life. He copied the manners of the world then passing before him, and has more allusions than other poets to the traditions and superstition of the vulgar ; which must therefore be traced before he can be understood.

He wrote at a time when our poetical language was yet unformed, when the meaning of our phrases was yet in fluctuation, when words were adopted at pleasure from the neighbouring languages, and while the *Saxon* was still visibly mingled in our diction. The reader is therefore embarrassed at once with dead and with foreign languages, with obsoleteness and innovation. In that age, as in all others, fashion produced phraseology, which succeeding fashion swept away before its meaning was generally known, or sufficiently authorized : and in that age, above all others, experiments were made upon our language, which distorted its combinations, and disturbed its uniformity.

If *Shakespeare* has difficulties above other writers, it is to be imputed to the nature of his work, which required the use of the common colloquial language, and consequently admitted many phrases allusive, elliptical, and proverbial, such as we speak and hear every hour without observing them ; and of which, being now familiar, we do not suspect that they can ever grow uncouth, or that, being now obvious, they can ever seem remote.

These are the principal causes of the obscurity of *Shakespeare* ; to which might be added that fulness of idea, which might sometimes load his words with more sentiment than they could conveniently convey, and that rapidity of imagination which might hurry him to a second thought before he had fully explained the first. But my opinion is, that very few of his lines were difficult to his audience, and that he used such expressions as were then common, though the paucity of contemporary writers makes them now seem peculiar.

Authors are often praised for improvement, or blamed for innovation, with very little justice, by those who read few other books of the same age. *Addison* himself has been so unsuccessful in enumerating the words with which *Milton* has enriched our language, as perhaps not to have named one of which *Milton* was the author ; and *Bentley* has yet more unhappily praised him as the introducer of those elisions into *English* poetry, which had been used from the first essays of versification among us, and which *Milton* was indeed the last that practised.

Another impediment, not the least vexatious to the commentator, is the exactness with which *Shakespeare* followed his authors. Instead of dilating his thoughts into generalities, and expressing incidents with poetical latitude, he often combines circumstances unnecessary to his main design, only because he happened to find them together. Such passages can be illustrated only by him who has read the same story in the very book which *Shakespeare* consulted.

He that undertakes an edition of *Shakespeare*, has all these difficulties to encounter, and all these obstructions to remove.

The corruptions of the text will be corrected by a careful collation of the oldest copies, by which it is hoped that many restorations may yet be made :

at least it will be necessary to collect and note the variations as materials for future criticks ; for it very often happens that a wrong reading has affinity to the right.

In this part all the present editions are apparently and intentionally defective. The criticks did not so much as wish to facilitate the labour of those that followed them. The same books are still to be compared ; the work that has been done, is to be done again ; and no single edition will supply the reader with a text on which he can rely as the best copy of the works of *Shakespeare*.

The edition now proposed will at least have this advantage over others. It will exhibit all the observable varieties of all the copies that can be found ; that, if the reader is not satisfied with the editor's determination, he may have the means of choosing better for himself.

Where all the books are evidently vitiated, and collation can give no assistance, then begins the task of critical sagacity : and some changes may well be admitted in a text never settled by the author, and so long exposed to caprice and ignorance. But nothing shall be imposed, as in the *Oxford* edition, without notice of the alteration ; nor shall conjecture be wantonly or unnecessarily indulged.

It has been long found, that very specious emendations do not equally strike all minds with conviction, nor even the same mind at different times ; and therefore, though perhaps many alterations may be proposed as eligible, very few will be obtruded as certain. In a language so ungrammatical as the *English*, and so licentious as that of *Shakespeare*, emendatory criticism is always hazardous ; nor can it be allowed to any man who is not particularly versed in the writings of that age, and particularly studious of his author's diction. There is danger lest peculiarities should be mistaken for corruptions, and passages rejected as unintelligible, which a narrow mind happens not to understand.

All the former criticks have been so much employed on the correction of the text, that they have not sufficiently attended to the elucidation of passages obscured by accident or time. The editor will endeavour to read the books which the author read, to trace his knowledge to its source, and compare his copies with their originals. If in this part of his design he hopes to attain any degree of superiority to his predecessors, it must be considered, that he has the advantage of their labours; that part of the work being already done, more care is naturally bestowed on the other part; and that, to declare the truth, Mr. *Rowe* and Mr. *Pope* were very ignorant of the ancient *English* literature; Dr. *Warburton* was detained by more important studies; and Mr. *Theobald*, if fame be just to his memory, considered learning only as an instrument of gain, and made no further inquiry after his author's meaning, when once he had notes sufficient to embellish his page with the expected decorations.

With regard to obsolete or peculiar diction, the editor may perhaps claim some degree of confidence, having had more motives to consider the whole extent of our language than any other man from its first formation. He hopes that, by comparing the works of *Shakespeare* with those of writers who lived at the same time, immediately preceded, or immediately followed him, he shall be able to ascertain his ambiguities, disentangle his intricacies, and recover the meaning of words now lost in the darkness of antiquity.

When therefore any obscurity arises from an allusion to some other book, the passage will be quoted. When

the diction is entangled, it will be cleared by a paraphrase or interpretation. When the sense is broken
by the suppression of part of the sentiment in pleasantry
or passion, the connexion will be supplied. When any
forgotten custom is hinted, care will be taken to retrieve
and explain it. The meaning assigned to doubtful
words will be supported by the authorities of other
writers, or by parallel passages of *Shakespeare* himself.

The observation of faults and beauties is one of the
duties of an annotator, which some of *Shakespeare*'s
editors have attempted, and some have neglected.
For this part of his task, and for this only, was Mr. *Pope*
eminently and indisputably qualified; nor has Dr.
Warburton followed him with less diligence or less
success. But I have never observed that mankind was
much delighted or improved by their asterisks, commas,
or double commas; of which the only effect is, that
they preclude the pleasure of judging for ourselves,
teach the young and ignorant to decide without
principles; defeat curiosity and discernment, by
leaving them less to discover; and at last show the
opinion of the critick, without the reasons on which
it was founded, and without affording any light by
which it may be examined.

The editor, though he may less delight his own
vanity will probably please his reader more, by supposing him equally able with himself to judge of
beauties and faults, which require no previous acquisition of remote knowledge. A description of the
obvious scenes of nature, a representation of general
life, a sentiment of reflection or experience, a deduction of conclusive argument, a forcible eruption of
effervescent passion, are to be considered as proportionate to common apprehension, unassisted by critical
officiousness; since, to conceive them, nothing more
is requisite than acquaintance with the general state

of the world, and those faculties which he must always bring with him who would read *Shakespeare*.

But when the beauty arises from some adaptation of the sentiment to customs worn out of use, to opinions not universally prevalent, or to any accidental or minute particularity, which cannot be supplied by common understanding, or common observation, it is the duty of a commentator to lend his assistance.

The notice of beauties and faults thus limited, will make no distinct part of the design, being reducible to the explanation of obscure passages.

The editor does not however intend to preclude himself from the comparison of *Shakespeare*'s sentiments or expression with those of ancient or modern authors, or from the display of any beauty not obvious to the students of poetry ; for as he hopes to leave his author better understood, he wishes likewise to procure him more rational approbation.

The former editors have affected to slight their predecessors : but in this edition all that is valuable will be adopted from every commentator, that posterity may consider it as including all the rest, and exhibiting whatever is hitherto known of the great father of the *English* drama.

PREFACE TO SHAKESPEARE

(1765)

THAT praises are without reason lavished on the dead, and that the honours due only to excellence are paid to antiquity, is a complaint likely to be always continued by those, who, being able to add nothing to truth, hope for eminence from the heresies of paradox; or those, who, being forced by disappointment upon consolatory expedients, are willing to hope from posterity what the present age refuses, and flatter themselves that the regard which is yet denied by envy, will be at last bestowed by time.

Antiquity, like every other quality that attracts the notice of mankind, has undoubtedly votaries that reverence it, not from reason, but from prejudice. Some seem to admire indiscriminately whatever has been long preserved, without considering that time has sometimes co-operated with chance; all perhaps are more willing to honour past than present excellence; and the mind contemplates genius through the shades of age, as the eye surveys the sun through artificial opacity. The great contention of criticism is to find the faults of the moderns, and the beauties of the ancients. While an authour is yet living we estimate his powers by his worst performance, and when he is dead, we rate them by his best.

To works, however, of which the excellence is not absolute and definite, but gradual and comparative; to works not raised upon principles demonstrative and scientifick, but appealing wholly to observation and experience, no other test can be applied than length of duration and continuance of esteem. What mankind have long possessed they have often examined and compared; and if they persist to value the possession, it is because frequent comparisons have confirmed opinion in its favour. As among the works of nature no man can properly call a river deep, or a mountain high, without the knowledge of many mountains, and many rivers; so in the productions of genius, nothing can be stiled excellent till it has been compared with other works of the same kind. Demonstration immediately displays its power, and has nothing to hope or fear from the flux of years; but works tentative and experimental must be estimated by their proportion to the general and collective ability of man, as it is discovered in a long succession of endeavours. Of the first building that was raised, it might be with certainty determined that it was round or square; but whether it was spacious or lofty must have been referred to time. The Pythagorean scale of numbers was at once discovered to be perfect; but the poems of *Homer* we yet know not to transcend the common limits of human intelligence, but by remarking, that nation after nation, and century after century, has been able to do little more than transpose his incidents, new-name his characters, and paraphrase his sentiments.

The reverence due to writings that have long subsisted arises therefore not from any credulous confidence in the superior wisdom of past ages, or gloomy persuasion of the degeneracy of mankind, but is the consequence of acknowledged and indubitable positions, that what has been longest known has been most considered, and what is most considered is best understood.

The Poet, of whose works I have undertaken the revision, may now begin to assume the dignity of an ancient, and claim the privilege of established fame and prescriptive veneration. He has long outlived his century, the term commonly fixed as the test of literary merit. Whatever advantages he might once derive from personal allusions, local customs, or temporary opinions, have for many years been lost; and every topick of merriment, or motive of sorrow, which the modes of artificial life afforded him, now only obscure the scenes which they once illuminated. The effects of favour and competition are at an end; the tradition of his friendships and his enmities has perished; his works support no opinion with arguments, nor supply any faction with invectives; they can neither indulge vanity nor gratify malignity; but are read without any other reason than the desire of pleasure, and are therefore praised only as pleasure is obtained; yet, thus unassisted by interest or passion, they have past through variations of taste and changes of manners, and, as they devolved from one generation to another, have received new honours at every transmission.

But because human judgment, though it be gradually gaining upon certainty, never becomes infallible; and approbation, though long continued, may yet be only the approbation of prejudice or fashion; it is proper to inquire, by what peculiarities of excellence *Shakespeare* has gained and kept the favour of his countrymen.

Nothing can please many, and please long, but just representations of general nature. Particular manners can be known to few, and therefore few only can judge how nearly they are copied. The irregular combinations of fanciful invention may delight a-while, by that novelty of which the common satiety of life sends us all in quest; but the pleasures of sudden wonder are soon exhausted, and the mind can only repose on the stability of truth.

Shakespeare is above all writers, at least above all modern writers, the poet of nature; the poet that holds up to his readers a faithful mirrour of manners and of life. His characters are not modified by the customs of particular places, unpractised by the rest of the world; by the peculiarities of studies or professions, which can operate but upon small numbers; or by the accidents of transient fashions or temporary opinions: they are the genuine progeny of common humanity, such as the world will always supply, and observation will always find. His persons act and speak by the influence of those general passions and principles by which all minds are agitated, and the whole system of life is continued in motion. In the writings of other poets a character is too often an individual; in those of *Shakespeare* it is commonly a species.

It is from this wide extension of design that so much instruction is derived. It is this which fills the plays of *Shakespeare* with practical axioms and domestick wisdom. It was said of *Euripides*, that every verse was a precept; and it may be said of *Shakespeare*, that from his works may be collected a system of civil and oeconomical prudence. Yet his real power is not shewn in the splendour of particular passages, but by the progress of his fable, and the tenour of his dialogue; and he that tries to recommend him by select quotations, will succeed like the pedant in *Hierocles*, who, when he offered his house to sale, carried a brick in his pocket as a specimen.

It will not easily be imagined how much *Shakespeare* excells in accommodating his sentiments to real life, but by comparing him with other authours. It was observed of the ancient schools of declamation, that the more diligently they were frequented, the more was the student disqualified for the world, because he found nothing there which he should ever meet in any other place. The same remark may be applied to every stage but that of *Shakespeare*. The theatre, when it is under any other direction, is peopled by such characters as were never seen, conversing in a language which was never heard, upon topicks which will never arise in the commerce of mankind. But the dialogue of this authour is often so evidently determined by the incident which produces it, and is pursued with so much ease and simplicity, that it seems scarcely to claim the merit of fiction, but to have been gleaned by diligent selection out of common conversation, and common occurrences.

Upon every other stage the universal agent is love, by whose power all good and evil is distributed, and every action quickened or retarded. To bring a lover, a lady and a rival into the fable; to entangle them in contradictory obligations, perplex them with oppositions of interest, and harrass them with violence of desires inconsistent with each other; to make them meet in rapture and part in agony; to fill their mouths with hyperbolical joy and outrageous sorrow; to distress them as nothing human ever was distressed; to deliver them as nothing human ever was delivered; is the business of a modern dramatist. For this probability is violated, life is misrepresented, and language is depraved. But love is only one of many passions; and as it has no great influence upon the sum of life, it has little operation in the dramas of a poet, who caught his ideas from the living world, and exhibited only what he saw before him. He knew, that any other passion, as it was regular or exorbitant, was a cause of happiness or calamity.

Characters thus ample and general were not easily discriminated and preserved, yet perhaps no poet ever kept his personages more distinct from each other. I will not say with *Pope*, that every speech may be assigned to the proper speaker, because many speeches there are which have nothing characteristical; but perhaps, though some may be equally adapted to every person, it will be difficult to find, any that can be properly transferred from the present possessor to another claimant. The choice is right, when there is reason for choice.

Other dramatists can only gain attention by hyperbolical or aggravated characters, by fabulous and unexampled excellence or depravity, as the writers of barbarous romances invigorated the reader by a giant and a dwarf; and he that should form his expectations of human affairs from the play, or from the tale, would be equally deceived. *Shakespeare* has no heroes; his scenes are occupied only by men, who act and speak as the reader thinks that he should himself have spoken or acted on the same occasion: Even where the agency is supernatural the dialogue is level with life. Other writers disguise the most natural passions and most frequent incidents; so that he who contemplates them in the book will not know them in the world: *Shakespeare* approximates the remote, and familiarizes the wonderful; the event which he represents will not happen, but if it were possible, its effects would probably be such as he has assigned; and it may be said, that he has not only shewn human nature as it acts in real exigencies, but as it would be found in trials, to which it cannot be exposed.

This therefore is the praise of *Shakespeare*, that his drama is the mirrour of life; that he who has mazed his imagination, in following the phantoms which other writers raise up before him, may here be cured of his delirious extasies, by reading human sentiments in human language, by scenes from which a hermit may estimate the transactions of the world, and a confessor predict the progress of the passions.

His adherence to general nature has exposed him to the censure of criticks, who form their judgments upon narrower principles. *Dennis* and *Rhymer* think his *Romans* not sufficiently *Roman*; and *Voltaire* censures his kings as not completely royal. *Dennis* is offended, that *Menenius*, a senator of *Rome*, should *play* the buffoon ; and *Voltaire* perhaps thinks decency violated when the *Danish* Usurper is represented as a drunkard. But *Shakespeare* always makes nature predominate over accident ; and if he preserves the essential character, is not very careful of distinctions superinduced and adventitious. His story requires Romans or kings, but he thinks only on men. He knew that *Rome*, like every other city, had men of all dispositions ; and wanting a buffoon, he went into the senate-house for that which the senate-house would certainly have afforded him. He was inclined to shew an usurper and a murderer not only odious but despicable, he therefore added drunkenness to his other qualities, knowing that kings love wine like other men, and that wine exerts its natural power upon kings. These are the petty cavils of petty minds ; a poet overlooks the casual distinction of country and condition, as a painter, satisfied with the figure, neglects the drapery.

The censure which he has incurred by mixing comick and tragick scenes, as it extends to all his works, deserves more consideration. Let the fact be first stated, and then examined.

Shakespeare's plays are not in the rigorous and critical sense either tragedies or comedies, but compositions of a distinct kind ; exhibiting the real state of sublunary nature, which partakes of good and evil, joy and sorrow, mingled with endless variety of proportion and innumerable modes of combination ; and expressing the course of the world, in which the loss of one is the gain of another ; in which, at the same time, the reveller is hasting to his wine, and the mourner burying his friend ; in which the malignity of one is sometimes defeated by the frolick of another ;

and many mischiefs and many benefits are done and hindered without design.

Out of this chaos of mingled purposes and casualties the ancient poets, according to the laws which custom had prescribed, selected some the crimes of men, and some their absurdities; some the momentous vicissitudes of life, and some the lighter occurrences; some the terrours of distress, and some the gayeties of prosperity. Thus rose the two modes of imitation, known by the names of *tragedy* and *comedy*, compositions intended to promote different ends by contrary means, and considered as so little allied, that I do not recollect among the *Greeks* or *Romans* a single writer who attempted both.

Shakespeare has united the powers of exciting laughter and sorrow not only in one mind, but in one composition. Almost all his plays are divided between serious and ludicrous characters, and, in the successive evolutions of the design, sometimes produce seriousness and sorrow, and sometimes levity and laughter.

That this is a practice contrary to the rules of criticism will be readily allowed; but there is always an appeal open from criticism to nature. The end of writing is to instruct; the end of poetry is to instruct by pleasing. That the mingled drama may convey all the instruction of tragedy or comedy cannot be denied, because it includes both in its alternations of exhibition and approaches nearer than either to the appearance of life, by shewing how great machinations and slender designs may promote or obviate one another, and the high and the low co-operate in the general system by unavoidable concatenation.

It is objected, that by this change of scenes the passions are interrupted in their progression, and that the principal event, being not advanced by a due gradation of preparatory incidents, wants at last the power to move, which constitutes the perfection of dramatick poetry. This reasoning is so specious, that it is received as true even by those who in daily experience feel it to be false. The interchanges of mingled scenes seldom fail to produce the intended vicissitudes of passion. Fiction cannot move so much, but that the attention may be easily transferred; and though it must be allowed that pleasing melancholy be sometimes interrupted by unwelcome levity, yet let it be considered likewise, that melancholy is often not pleasing, and that the disturbance of one man may be the relief of another; that different auditors have different habitudes; and that, upon the whole, all pleasure consists in variety.

The players, who in their edition divided our authour's works into comedies, histories, and tragedies, seem not to have distinguished the three kinds by any very exact or definite ideas.

An action which ended happily to the principal persons, however serious or distressful through its intermediate incidents, in their opinion, constituted a comedy. This idea of a comedy continued long amongst us; and plays were written, which, by changing the catastrophe, were tragedies to-day, and comedies to-morrow.

Tragedy was not in those times a poem of more general dignity or elevation than comedy; it required only a calamitous conclusion, with which the common criticism of that age was satisfied, whatever lighter pleasure it afforded in its progress.

History was a series of actions, with no other than chronological succession, independent on each other, and without any tendency to introduce or regulate the conclusion. It is not always very nicely distinguished from tragedy. There is not much nearer approach to unity of action in the tragedy of *Antony and Cleopatra,* than in the history of *Richard the Second.* But a history might be continued through many plays ; as it had no plan, it had no limits.

Through all these denominations of the drama, *Shakespeare's* mode of composition is the same ; an interchange of seriousness and merriment, by which the mind is softened at one time, and exhilarated at another. But whatever be his purpose, whether to gladden or depress, or to conduct the story, without vehemence or emotion, through tracts of easy and familiar dialogue, he never fails to attain his purpose ; as he commands us, we laugh or mourn, or sit silent with quiet expectation, in tranquillity without indifference.

When *Shakespeare's* plan is understood, most of the criticisms of *Rhymer* and *Voltaire* vanish away. The play of *Hamlet* is opened, without impropriety, by two sentinels ; *Iago* bellows at *Brabantio's* window, without injury to the scheme of the play, though in terms which a modern audience would not easily endure ; the character of *Polonius* is seasonable and useful ; and the Grave-diggers themselves may be heard with applause.

Shakespeare engaged in dramatick poetry with the world open before him ; the rules of the ancients were yet known to few ; the publick judgment was unformed ; he had no example of such fame as might force him upon imitation, nor criticks of such authority as might restrain his extravagance : He therefore indulged his natural disposition, and his disposition, as *Rhymer* has remarked, led him to comedy. In tragedy he often writes, with great appearance of toil and study, what is written at last with little felicity ; but in his comick scenes, he seems to produce without labour, what no labour can improve. In tragedy he is always struggling after some occasion to be comick ;

but in comedy he seems to repose, or to luxuriate, as in a mode of thinking congenial to his nature. In his tragick scenes there is always something wanting, but his comedy often surpasses expectation or desire. His comedy pleases by the thoughts and the language, and his tragedy for the greater part by incident and action. His tragedy seems to be skill, his comedy to be instinct.

The force of his comick scenes has suffered little diminution from the changes made by a century and a half, in manners or in words. As his personages act upon principles arising from genuine passion, very little modified by particular forms, their pleasures and vexations are communicable to all times and to all places; they are natural, and therefore durable; the adventitious peculiarities of personal habits, are only superficial dies, bright and pleasing for a little while, yet soon fading to a dim tinct, without any remains of former lustre; but the discriminations of true passion are the colours of nature; they pervade the whole mass, and can only perish with the body that exhibits them. The accidental compositions of heterogeneous modes are dissolved by the chance which combined them; but the uniform simplicity of primitive qualities neither admits increase, nor suffers decay. The sand heaped by one flood is scattered by another, but the rock always continues in its place. The stream of time, which is continually washing the dissoluble fabricks of other poets, passes without injury by the adamant of *Shakespeare*.

If there be, what I believe there is, in every nation, a stile which never becomes obsolete, a certain mode of phraseology so consonant and congenial to the analogy and principles of its respective language as to remain settled and unaltered; this style is probably to be sought in the common intercourse of life, among those who speak only to be understood, without ambition of elegance. The polite are always catching modish innovations, and the learned depart from established forms of speech, in hope of finding or making better ; those who wish for distinction forsake the vulgar, when the vulgar is right ; but there is a conversation above grossness and below refinement, where propriety resides, and where this poet seems to have gathered his comick dialogue. He is therefore more agreeable to the ears of the present age than any other authour equally remote, and among his other excellencies deserves to be studied as one of the original masters of our language.

These observations are to be considered not as unexceptionably constant, but as containing general and predominant truth. *Shakespeare*'s familiar dialogue is affirmed to be smooth and clear, yet not wholly without ruggedness or difficulty ; as a country may be eminently fruitful, though it has spots unfit for cultivation : His characters are praised as natural, though their sentiments are sometimes forced, and their actions improbable ; as the earth upon the whole is spherical, though its surface is varied with protuberances and cavities.

Shakespeare with his excellencies has likewise faults, and faults sufficient to obscure and overwhelm any other merit. I shall shew them in the proportion in which they appear to me, without envious malignity or superstitious veneration. No question can be more innocently discussed than a dead poet's pretensions to renown ; and little regard is due to that bigotry which sets candour higher than truth.

His first defect is that to which may be imputed most of the evil in books or in men. He sacrifices virtue to convenience, and is so much more careful to please than to instruct, that he seems to write

without any moral purpose.   From his writings indeed
a system of social duty may be selected, for he that
thinks reasonably must think morally ; but his precepts
and axioms drop casually from him ; he makes no just
distribution of good or evil, nor is always careful to
shew in the virtuous a disapprobation of the wicked ;
he carries his persons indifferently through right and
wrong, and at the close dismisses them without further
care, and leaves their examples to operate by chance.
This fault the barbarity of his age cannot extenuate ;
for it is always a writer's duty to make the world
better, and justice is a virtue independant on time or
place.

The plots are often so loosely formed, that a very
slight consideration may improve them, and so carelessly pursued, that he seems not always fully to comprehend his own design. He omits opportunities of
instructing or delighting which the train of his story
seems to force upon him, and apparently rejects those
exhibitions which would be more affecting, for the
sake of those which are more easy.

It may be observed, that in many of his plays the
latter part is evidently neglected. When he found
himself near the end of his work, and, in view of his
reward, he shortened the labour to snatch the profit.
He therefore remits his efforts where he should most
vigorously exert them, and his catastrophe is impro-
bably produced or imperfectly represented.

He had no regard to distinction of time or place,
but gives to one age or nation, without scruple, the
customs, institutions, and opinions of another, at the
expence not only of likelihood, but of possibility.
These faults *Pope* has endeavoured, with more zeal
than judgment, to transfer to his imagined interpo-
lators. We need not wonder to find *Hector* quoting
Aristotle, when we see the loves of *Theseus* and *Hippo-*

lyta combined with the *Gothick* mythology of fairies. *Shakespeare*, indeed, was not the only violator of chronology, for in the same age *Sidney*, who wanted not the advantages of learning, has, in his *Arcadia*, confounded the pastoral with the feudal times, the days of innocence, quiet and security, with those of turbulence, violence, and adventure.

In his comick scenes he is seldom very successful, when he engages his characters in reciprocations of smartness and contests of sarcasm ; their jests are commonly gross, and their pleasantry licentious ; neither his gentlemen nor his ladies have much delicacy, nor are sufficiently distinguished from his clowns by any appearance of refined manners. Whether he represented the real conversation of his time is not easy to determine ; the reign of *Elizabeth* is commonly supposed to have been a time of stateliness, formality and reserve ; yet perhaps the relaxations of that severity were not very elegant. There must, however, have been always some modes of gayety preferable to others, and a writer ought to chuse the best.

In tragedy his performance seems constantly to be worse, as his labour is more. The effusions of passion which exigence forces out are for the most part striking and energetick ; but whenever he solicits his invention, or strains his faculties, the offspring of his throes is tumour, meanness, tediousness, and obscurity.

In narration he affects a disproportionate pomp of diction, and a wearisome train of circumlocution, and tells the incident imperfectly in many words, which might have been more plainly delivered in few. Narration in dramatick poetry is naturally tedious, as it is unanimated and inactive, and obstructs the progress of the action ; it should therefore always be rapid, and enlivened by frequent interruption. *Shakespeare* found it an encumbrance, and instead of lightening it by brevity, endeavoured to recommend it by dignity and splendour.

His declamations or set speeches are commonly cold and weak, for his power was the power of nature; when he endeavoured, like other tragick writers, to catch opportunities of amplification, and instead of inquiring what the occasion demanded, to show how much his stores of knowledge could supply, he seldom escapes without the pity or resentment of his reader.

It is incident to him to be now and then entangled with an unwieldy sentiment, which he cannot well express, and will not reject; he struggles with it a while, and if it continues stubborn, comprises it in words such as occur, and leaves it to be disentangled and evolved by those who have more leisure to bestow upon it.

Not that always where the language is intricate the thought is subtle, or the image always great where the line is bulky; the equality of words to things is very often neglected, and trivial sentiments and vulgar ideas disappoint the attention, to which they are recommended by sonorous epithets and swelling figures.

But the admirers of this great poet have never less reason to indulge their hopes of supreme excellence, than when he seems fully resolved to sink them in dejection, and mollify them with tender emotions by the fall of greatness, the danger of innocence, or the crosses of love. He is not long soft and pathetick without some idle conceit, or contemptible equivocation. He no sooner begins to move, than he counteracts himself; and terrour and pity, as they are rising in the mind, are checked and blasted by sudden frigidity.

A quibble is to *Shakespeare*, what luminous vapours are to the traveller; he follows it at all adventures; it is sure to lead him out of his way, and sure to engulf

him in the mire. It has some malignant power over
his mind, and its fascinations are irresistible. Whatever
be the dignity or profundity of his disquisition, whether
he be enlarging knowledge or exalting affection,
whether he be amusing attention with incidents, or
enchaining it in suspense, let but a quibble spring
up before him, and he leaves his work unfinished.
A quibble is the golden apple for which he will always
turn aside from his career, or stoop from his elevation.
A quibble, poor and barren as it is, gave him such
delight, that he was content to purchase it, by the
sacrifice of reason, propriety and truth. A quibble
was to him the fatal *Cleopatra* for which he lost the
world, and was content to lose it.

It will be thought strange, that, in enumerating the
defects of this writer, I have not yet mentioned his
neglect of the unities ; his violation of those laws
which have been instituted and established by the
joint authority of poets and of criticks.

For his other deviations from the art of writing
I resign him to critical justice, without making any
other demand in his favour, than that which must
be indulged to all human excellence : that his virtues
be rated with his failings : But, from the censure which
this irregularity may bring upon him, I shall, with
due reverence to that learning which I must oppose,
adventure to try how I can defend him.

His histories, being neither tragedies nor comedies
are not subject to any of their laws ; nothing more is
necessary to all the praise which they expect, than that
the changes of action be so prepared as to be understood, that the incidents be various and affecting,
and the characters consistent, natural, and distinct.
No other unity is intended, and therefore none is to
be sought.

In his other works he has well enough preserved the

unity of action. He has not, indeed, an intrigue regularly perplexed and regularly unravelled : he does not endeavour to hide his design only to discover it, for this is seldom the order of real events, and *Shakespeare* is the poet of nature : But his plan has commonly what *Aristotle* requires, a beginning, a middle, and an end ; one event is concatenated with another, and the conclusion follows by easy consequence. There are perhaps some incidents that might be spared, as in other poets there is much talk that only fills up time upon the stage ; but the general system makes gradual advances, and the end of the play is the end of expectation.

To the unities of time and place he has shewn no regard ; and perhaps a nearer view of the principles on which they stand will diminish their value, and withdraw from them the veneration which, from the time of *Corneille*, they have very generally received, by discovering that they have given more trouble to the poet, than pleasure to the auditor.

The necessity of observing the unities of time and place arises from the supposed necessity of making the drama credible. The criticks hold it impossible, that an action of months or years can be possibly believed to pass in three hours ; or that the spectator can suppose himself to sit in the theatre, while ambassadors go and return between distant kings, while armies are levied and towns besieged, while an exile wanders and returns, or till he whom they saw courting his mistress, shall lament the untimely fall of his son. The mind revolts from evident falsehood, and fiction loses its force when it departs from the resemblance of reality.

From the narrow limitation of time necessarily arises the contraction of place. The spectator, who knows that he saw the first act at *Alexandria*, cannot suppose that he sees the next at *Rome*, at a distance to which not the dragons of *Medea* could, in so short a time, have transported him ; he knows with certainty that he has not changed his place, and he knows that place cannot change itself ; that what was a house cannot become a plain ; that what was *Thebes* can never be *Persepolis.*

Such is the triumphant language with which a critick exults over the misery of an irregular poet, and exults commonly without resistance or reply. It is time therefore to tell him by the authority of *Shakespeare,* that he assumes, as an unquestionable principle, a position, which, while his breath is forming it into words, his understanding pronounces to be false. It is false, that any representation is mistaken for reality ; that any dramatick fable in its materiality was ever credible, or, for a single moment, was ever credited.

The objection arising from the impossibility of passing the first hour at *Alexandria,* and the next at *Rome,* supposes, that when the play opens, the spectator really imagines himself at *Alexandria,* and believes that his walk to the theatre has been a voyage to *Egypt,* and that he lives in the days of *Antony* and *Cleopatra.* Surely he that imagines this may imagine more. He that can take the stage at one time for the palace of the *Ptolemies,* may take it in half an hour for the promontory of *Actium.* Delusion, if delusion be admitted, has no certain limitation ; if the spectator can be once persuaded, that his old acquaintance are *Alexander* and *Cæsar,* that a room illuminated with candles is the plain of *Pharsalia,* or the bank of *Granicus,* he is in a state of elevation above the reach of reason, or of truth, and from the heights of empyrean poetry, may despise the circumscriptions of terrestrial nature. There is no reason why a mind thus wandering in extasy should count the clock, or why an hour should not be a century in that calenture of the brains that can make the stage a field.

The truth is, that the spectators are always in their senses, and know, from the first act to the last, that the stage is only a stage, and that the players are only players. They came to hear a certain number of lines recited with just gesture and elegant modulation. The lines relate to some action, and an action must be in some place; but the different actions that compleat a story may be in places very remote from each other; and where is the absurdity of allowing that space to represent first *Athens*, and then *Sicily*, which was always known to be neither *Sicily* nor *Athens*, but a modern theatre?

By supposition, as place is introduced, time may be extended; the time required by the fable elapses for the most part between the acts; for, of so much of the action as is represented, the real and poetical duration is the same. If, in the first act, preparations for war against *Mithridates* are represented to be made in *Rome*, the event of the war may, without absurdity, be represented, in the catastrophe, as happening in *Pontus*; we know that there is neither war, nor preparation for war; we know that we are neither in *Rome* nor *Pontus*; that neither *Mithridates* nor *Lucullus* are before us. The drama exhibits successive imitations of successive actions; and why may not the second imitation represent an action that happened years after the first, if it be so connected with it, that nothing but time can be supposed to intervene? Time is, of all modes of existence, most obsequious to the imagination; a lapse of years is as easily conceived as a passage of hours. In contemplation we easily contract the time of real actions, and therefore willingly permit it to be contracted when we only see their imitation.

It will be asked, how the drama moves, if it is not credited. It is credited with all the credit due to a drama. It is credited, whenever it moves, as a just picture of a real original; as representing to the auditor what he would himself feel, if he were to do or suffer what is there feigned to be suffered or to be done. The reflection that strikes the heart is not, that the evils before us are real evils, but that they are evils to which we ourselves may be exposed. If there be any fallacy, it is not that we fancy the players, but that we fancy ourselves unhappy for a moment; but we rather lament the possibility than suppose the presence of misery, as a mother weeps over her babe, when she remembers that death may take it from her. The delight of tragedy proceeds from our consciousness of fiction; if we thought murders and treasons real, they would please no more.

Imitations produce pain or pleasure, not because they are mistaken for realities, but because they bring realities to mind. When the imagination is recreated by a painted landscape, the trees are not supposed capable to give us shade, or the fountains coolness; but we consider, how we should be pleased with such fountains playing beside us, and such woods waving over us. We are agitated in reading the history of *Henry* the Fifth, yet no man takes his book for the field of *Agencourt*. A dramatick exhibition is a book recited with concomitants that encrease or diminish its effect. Familiar comedy is often more powerful on the theatre, than in the page; imperial tragedy is always less. The humour of *Petruchio* may be heightened by grimace; but what voice or what gesture can hope to add dignity or force to the soliloquy of *Cato*.

A play read, affects the mind like a play acted. It is therefore evident, that the action is not supposed to be real; and it follows, that between the acts

a longer or shorter time may be allowed to pass, and
that no more account of space or duration is to be
taken by the auditor of a drama, than by the reader
of a narrative, before whom may pass in an hour the
life of a hero, or the revolutions of an empire.

Whether *Shakespeare* knew the unities, and rejected
them by design, or deviated from them by happy
ignorance, it is, I think, impossible to decide, and
useless to enquire. We may reasonably suppose, that,
when he rose to notice, he did not want the counsels
and admonitions of scholars and criticks, and that he
at last deliberately persisted in a practice, which he
might have begun by chance. As nothing is essential
to the fable, but unity of action, and as the unities of
time and place arise evidently from false assumptions,
and, by circumscribing the extent of the drama,
lessen its variety, I cannot think it much to be lamented,
that they were not known by him, or not observed :
Nor, if such another poet could arise, should I very
vehemently reproach him, that his first act passed at
Venice, and his next in *Cyprus*. Such violations of
rules merely positive, become the comprehensive genius
of *Shakespeare*, and such censures are suitable to the
minute and slender criticism of *Voltaire :*

> *Non usque adeo permiscuit imis*
> *Longus summa dies, ut non, si voce Metelli*
> *Serventur leges, malint a Cæsare tolli.*

Yet when I speak thus slightly of dramatick rules,
I cannot but recollect how much wit and learning
may be produced against me ; before such authorities
I am afraid to stand, not that I think the present
question one of those that are to be decided by mere
authority, but because it is to be suspected, that these
precepts have not been so easily received but for
better reasons than I have yet been able to find. The

result of my enquiries, in which it would be ludicrous to boast of impartiality, is, that the unities of time and place are not essential to a just drama, that though they may sometimes conduce to pleasure, they are always to be sacrificed to the nobler beauties of variety and instruction ; and that a play, written with nice observation of critical rules, is to be contemplated as an elaborate curiosity, as the product of superfluous and ostentatious art, by which is shewn, rather what is possible, than what is necessary.

He that, without diminution of any other excellence, shall preserve all the unities unbroken, deserves the like applause with the architect, who shall display all the orders of architecture in a citadel, without any deduction from its strength ; but the principal beauty of a citadel is to exclude the enemy ; and the greatest graces of a play, are to copy nature and instruct life.

Perhaps, what I have here not dogmatically but deliberately written, may recal the principles of the drama to a new examination. I am almost frighted at my own temerity ; and when I estimate the fame and the strength of those that maintain the contrary opinion, am ready to sink down in reverential silence ; as *Æneas* withdrew from the defence of *Troy*, when he saw *Neptune* shaking the wall, and *Juno* heading the besiegers.

Those whom my arguments cannot persuade to give their approbation to the judgment of *Shakespeare*, will easily, if they consider the condition of his life, make some allowance for his ignorance.

Every man's performances, to be rightly estimated, must be compared with the state of the age in which he lived, and with his own particular opportunities ; and though to the reader a book be not worse or better for the circumstances of the authour, yet as there is always a silent reference of human works to human abilities, and as the enquiry, how far man may extend his designs, or how high he may rate his native force, is of far greater dignity than in what rank we shall place any particular performance, curiosity is always busy to discover the instruments, as well as to survey the workmanship, to know how much is to be ascribed to original powers, and how much to casual and adventitious help. The palaces of *Peru* or *Mexico* were certainly mean and incommodious habitations, if compared to the houses of *European* monarchs; yet who could forbear to view them with astonishment, who remembered that they were built without the use of iron?

The *English* nation, in the time of *Shakespeare*, was yet struggling to emerge from barbarity. The philology of *Italy* had been transplanted hither in the reign of *Henry* the Eighth; and the learned languages had been successfully cultivated by *Lilly*, *Linacer*, and *More*; by *Pole*, *Cheke*, and *Gardiner*; and afterwards by *Smith*, *Clerk*, *Haddon*, and *Ascham*. Greek was now taught to boys in the principal schools; and those who united elegance with learning, read, with great diligence, the *Italian* and *Spanish* poets. But literature was yet confined to professed scholars, or to men and women of high rank. The publick was gross and dark; and to be able to read and write, was an accomplishment still valued for its rarity

Nations, like individuals, have their infancy. A people newly awakened to literary curiosity, being yet unacquainted with the true state of things, knows not how to judge of that which is proposed as its resemblance. Whatever is remote from common appearances is always welcome to vulgar, as to childish credulity; and of a country unenlightened by learning, the whole people is the vulgar. The study of those who then aspired to plebeian learning was laid out

upon adventures, giants, dragons, and enchantments.
The Death of Arthur was the favourite volume.

The mind, which has feasted on the luxurious wonders of fiction, has no taste of the insipidity of truth.
A play which imitated only the common occurrences
of the world, would, upon the admirers of *Palmerin*
and *Guy* of *Warwick*, have made little impression; he
that wrote for such an audience was under the necessity
of looking round for strange events and fabulous transactions, and that incredibility, by which maturer
knowledge is offended, was the chief recommendation
of writings, to unskilful curiosity.

Our authour's plots are generally borrowed from
novels, and it is reasonable to suppose, that he chose
the most popular, such as were read by many, and
related by more; for his audience could not have
followed him through the intricacies of the drama,
had they not held the thread of the story in their
hands.

The stories, which we now find only in remoter
authours, were in his time accessible and familiar.
The fable of *As you like it*, which is supposed to be
copied from *Chaucer's* Gamelyn, was a little pamphlet
of those times; and old Mr. *Cibber* remembered the
tale of *Hamlet* in plain *English* prose, which the
criticks have now to seek in *Saxo Grammaticus*.

His *English* histories he took from *English* chronicles
and *English* ballads; and as the ancient writers were
made known to his countrymen by versions, they
supplied him with new subjects; he dilated some of
Plutarch's lives into plays, when they had been translated by *North*.

His plots, whether historical or fabulous, are always
crouded with incidents, by which the attention of
a rude people was more easily caught than by sentiment or argumentation; and such is the power of the

marvellous even over those who despise it, that every man finds his mind more strongly seized by the tragedies of *Shakespeare* than of any other writer; others please us by particular speeches, but he always makes us anxious for the event, and has perhaps excelled all but *Homer* in securing the first purpose of a writer, by exciting restless and unquenchable curiosity and compelling him that reads his work to read it through.

The shows and bustle with which his plays abound have the same original. As knowledge advances, pleasure passes from the eye to the ear, but returns, as it declines, from the ear to the eye. Those to whom our authour's labours were exhibited had more skill in pomps or processions than in poetical language, and perhaps wanted some visible and discriminated events, as comments on the dialogue. He knew how he should most please; and whether his practice is more agreeable to nature, or whether his example has prejudiced the nation, we still find that on our stage something must be done as well as said, and inactive declamation is very coldly heard, however musical or elegant, passionate or sublime.

Voltaire expresses his wonder, that our authour's extravagances are endured by a nation, which has seen the tragedy of *Cato*. Let him be answered, that *Addison* speaks the language of poets, and *Shakespeare*, of men. We find in *Cato* innumerable beauties which enamour us of its authour, but we see nothing that acquaints us with human sentiments or human actions; we place it with the fairest and the noblest progeny which judgment propagates by conjunction with learning, but *Othello* is the vigorous and vivacious offspring of observation impregnated by genius. *Cato* affords a splendid exhibition of artificial and fictitious manners, and delivers just and noble sentiments, in diction easy, elevated and harmonious, but its hopes and fears communicate no vibration to the heart; the composition refers us only to the writer; we pronounce the name of *Cato*, but we think on *Addison*.

The work of a correct and regular writer is a garden accurately formed and diligently planted, varied with shades, and scented with flowers; the composition of *Shakespeare* is a forest, in which oaks extend their branches, and pines tower in the air, interspersed sometimes with weeds and brambles, and sometimes giving shelter to myrtles and to roses; filling the eye with awful pomp, and gratifying the mind with endless diversity. Other poets display cabinets of precious rarities, minutely finished, wrought into shape, and polished unto brightness. *Shakespeare* opens a mine which contains gold and diamonds in unexhaustible plenty, though clouded by incrustations, debased by impurities, and mingled with a mass of meaner minerals.

It has been much disputed, whether *Shakespeare* owed his excellence to his own native force, or whether he had the common helps of scholastick education, the precepts of critical science, and the examples of ancient authours.

There has always prevailed a tradition, that *Shakespeare* wanted learning, that he had no regular education, nor much skill in the dead languages. *Johnson*, his friend, affirms, that *he had small Latin, and no Greek*; who, besides that he had no imaginable temptation to falsehood, wrote at a time when the character and acquisitions of *Shakespeare* were known to multitudes. His evidence ought therefore to decide the controversy, unless some testimony of equal force could be opposed.

Some have imagined, that they have discovered deep learning in many imitations of old writers; but

the examples which I have known urged, were drawn
from books translated in his time; or were such easy
coincidencies of thought, as will happen to all who
consider the same subjects; or such remarks on life
or axioms of morality as float in conversation, and are
transmitted through the world in proverbial sentences.

I have found it remarked, that, in this important
sentence, *Go before, I'll follow*, we read a translation
of, *I prae, sequar*. I have been told, that when
Caliban, after a pleasing dream, says, *I cry'd to sleep
again*, the authour imitates *Anacreon*, who had, like
every other man, the same wish on the same occasion.

There are a few passages which may pass for imitations, but so few, that the exception only confirms
the rule; he obtained them from accidental quotations, or by oral communication, and as he used what
he had, would have used more if he had obtained it.

The *Comedy of Errors* is confessedly taken from the
Menæchmi of *Plautus*; from the only play of *Plautus*
which was then in *English*. What can be more probable, than that he who copied that, would have
copied more; but that those which were not translated
were inaccessible?

Whether he knew the modern languages is uncertain.
That his plays have some *French* scenes proves but little;
he might easily procure them to be written, and probably, even though he had known the language in the
common degree, he could not have written it without
assistance. In the story of *Romeo* and *Juliet* he is
observed to have followed the *English* translation,
where it deviates from the *Italian*; but this on the
other part proves nothing against his knowledge of
the original. He was to copy, not what he knew
himself, but what was known to his audience.

It is most likely that he had learned *Latin* sufficiently
to make him acquainted with construction, but that

he never advanced to an easy perusal of the *Roman* authours. Concerning his skill in modern languages, I can find no sufficient ground of determination; but as no imitations of *French* or *Italian* authours have been discovered, though the *Italian* poetry was then high in esteem, I am inclined to believe, that he read little more than *English*, and chose for his fables only such tales as he found translated.

That much knowledge is scattered over his works is very justly observed by *Pope*, but it is often such knowledge as books did not supply. He that will understand *Shakespeare*, must not be content to study him in the closet, he must look for his meaning sometimes among the sports of the field, and sometimes among the manufactures of the shop.

There is however proof enough that he was a very diligent reader, nor was our language then so indigent of books, but that he might very liberally indulge his curiosity without excursion into foreign literature. Many of the *Roman* authours were translated, and some of the *Greek*; the reformation had filled the kingdom with theological learning; most of the topicks of human disquisition had found *English* writers; and poetry had been cultivated, not only with diligence, but success. This was a stock of knowledge sufficient for a mind so capable of appropriating and improving it.

But the greater part of his excellence was the product of his own genius. He found the *English* stage in a state of the utmost rudeness; no essays either in tragedy or comedy had appeared, from which it could be discovered to what degree of delight either one or other might be carried. Neither character nor dialogue were yet understood. *Shakespeare* may be truly said to have introduced them both amongst us, and in some of his happier scenes to have carried them both to the utmost height.

By what gradations of improvement he proceeded, is not easily known; for the chronology of his works is yet unsettled. *Rowe* is of opinion, that *perhaps we are not to look for his beginning, like those of other writers, in his least perfect works; art had so little, and nature so large a share in what he did, that for ought I know,* says he, *the performances of his youth, as they were the most vigorous, were the best.* But the power of nature is only the power of using to any certain purpose the materials which diligence procures, or opportunity supplies. Nature gives no man knowledge, and when images are collected by study and experience, can only assist in combining or applying them. *Shakespeare*, however favoured by nature, could impart only what he had learned; and as he must increase his ideas, like other mortals, by gradual acquisition, he, like them, grew wiser as he grew older, could display life better, as he knew it more, and instruct with more efficacy, as he was himself more amply instructed.

There is a vigilance of observation and accuracy of distinction which books and precepts cannot confer; from this almost all original and native excellence proceeds. *Shakespeare* must have looked upon mankind with perspicacity, in the highest degree curious and attentive. Other writers borrow their characters from preceding writers, and diversify them only by the accidental appendages of present manners; the dress is a little varied, but the body is the same. Our authour had both matter and form to provide; for except the characters of *Chaucer*, to whom I think he is not much indebted, there were no writers in *English*, and perhaps not many in other modern languages, which shewed life in its native colours.

The contest about the original benevolence or malignity of man had not yet commenced. Speculation had not yet attempted to analyse the mind, to trace the passions to their sources, to unfold the seminal principles of vice and virtue, or sound the depths of the heart for the motives of action. All those enquiries, which from that time that human nature became the fashionable study, have been made sometimes with nice discernment, but often with idle subtilty, were yet unattempted. The tales, with which the infancy of learning was satisfied, exhibited only the superficial appearances of action, related the events but omitted the causes, and were formed for such as delighted in wonders rather than in truth. Mankind was not then to be studied in the closet; he that would know the world, was under the necessity of gleaning his own remarks, by mingling as he could in its business and amusements.

Boyle congratulated himself upon his high birth, because it favoured his curiosity, by facilitating his access. *Shakespeare* had no such advantage; he came to *London* a needy adventurer, and lived for a time by very mean employments. Many works of genius and learning have been performed in states of life, that appear very little favourable to thought or to enquiry; so many, that he who considers them is inclined to think that he sees enterprise and perseverance predominating over all external agency, and bidding help and hindrance vanish before them. The genius of *Shakespeare* was not to be depressed by the weight of poverty, nor limited by the narrow conversation to which men in want are inevitably condemned; the incumbrances of his fortune were shaken from his mind, *as dewdrops from a lion's mane.*

Though he had so many difficulties to encounter, and so little assistance to surmount them, he has been able to obtain an exact knowledge of many modes of life, and many casts of native dispositions; to vary them with great multiplicity; to mark them by nice distinctions; and to shew them in full view by proper combinations. In this part of his performances he had none to imitate, but has himself been imitated by all succeeding writers; and it may be doubted, whether from all his successors more maxims of theoretical knowledge, or more rules of practical prudence, can be collected, than he alone has given to his country.

Nor was his attention confined to the actions of men; he was an exact surveyor of the inanimate world; his descriptions have always some peculiarities, gathered by contemplating things as they really exist. It may be observed, that the oldest poets of many nations preserve their reputation, and that the following generations of wit, after a short celebrity, sink into oblivion. The first, whoever they be, must take their sentiments and descriptions immediately from knowledge; the resemblance is therefore just, their descriptions are verified by every eye, and their sentiments acknowledged by every breast. Those whom their fame invites to the same studies, copy partly them, and partly nature, till the books of one age gain such authority, as to stand in the place of nature to another, and imitation, always deviating a little, becomes at last capricious and casual. *Shakespeare*, whether life or nature be his subject, shews plainly, that he has seen with his own eyes; he gives the image which he receives, not weakened or distorted by the intervention of any other mind; the ignorant feel his representations to be just, and the learned see that they are compleat.

Perhaps it would not be easy to find any authour, except *Homer*, who invented so much as *Shakespeare*, who so much advanced the studies which he cultivated, or effused so much novelty upon his age or country. The form, the characters, the language, and the shows of the *English* drama are his. *He seems*, says *Dennis*, *to have been the very original of our* English *tragical harmony, that is, the harmony of blank verse, diversified often by dissyllable and trissyllable terminations. For the diversity distinguishes it from heroick harmony, and by bringing it nearer to common use makes it more proper to gain attention, and more fit for action and dialogue. Such verse we make when we are writing prose ; we make such verse in common conversation.*

I know not whether this praise is rigorously just. The dissyllable termination, which the critick rightly appropriates to the drama, is to be found, though, I think, not in *Gorboduc* which is confessedly before our authour ; yet in *Hieronnymo*, of which the date is not certain, but which there is reason to believe at least as old as his earliest plays. This however is certain, that he is the first who taught either tragedy or comedy to please, there being no theatrical piece of any older writer, of which the name is known, except to antiquaries and collectors of books, which are sought because they are scarce, and would not have been scarce, had they been much esteemed.

To him we must ascribe the praise, unless *Spenser* may divide it with him, of having first discovered to how much smoothness and harmony the *English* language could be softened. He has speeches, perhaps sometimes scenes, which have all the delicacy of *Rowe*, without his effeminacy. He endeavours indeed commonly to strike by the force and vigour of his dialogue, but he never executes his purpose better, than when he tries to sooth by softness.

Yet it must be at last confessed, that as we owe every thing to him, he owes something to us ; that, if much of his praise is paid by perception and judgement, much is likewise given by custom and veneration. We fix our eyes upon his graces, and turn them from his deformities, and endure in him what we should in another loath or despise. If we endured without praising, respect for the father of our drama might excuse us ; but I have seen, in the book of some modern critick, a collection of anomalies, which shew that he has corrupted language by every mode of depravation, but which his admirer has accumulated as a monument of honour.

He has scenes of undoubted and perpetual excellence, but perhaps not one play, which, if it were now exhibited as the work of a contemporary writer, would be heard to the conclusion. I am indeed far from thinking, that his works were wrought to his own ideas of perfection ; when they were such as would satisfy the audience, they satisfied the writer. It is seldom that authours, though more studious of fame than *Shakespeare*, rise much above the standard of their own age ; to add a little of what is best will always be sufficient for present praise, and those who find themselves exalted into fame, are willing to credit their encomiasts, and to spare the labour of contending with themselves.

It does not appear, that *Shakespeare* thought his works worthy of posterity, that he levied any ideal tribute upon future times, or had any further prospect, than of present popularity and present profit. When his plays had been acted, his hope was at an end ; he solicited no addition of honour from the reader. He therefore made no scruple to repeat the same jests in many dialogues, or to entangle different plots by the same knot of perplexity, which may be at least forgiven him, by those who recollect, that of *Congreve*'s four comedies, two are concluded by a marriage in a mask, by a deception, which perhaps never happened, and which, whether likely or not, he did not invent.

So careless was this great poet of future fame, that, though he retired to ease and plenty, while he was yet little *declined into the vale of years*, before he could be disgusted with fatigue, or disabled by infirmity, he made no collection of his works, nor desired to rescue those that had been already published from the depravations that obscured them, or secure to the rest a better destiny, by giving them to the world in their genuine state.

Of the plays which bear the name of *Shakespeare* in the late editions, the greater part were not published till about seven years after his death, and the few which appeared in his life are apparently thrust into the world without the care of the authour, and therefore probably without his knowledge.

Of all the publishers, clandestine or professed, their negligence and unskilfulness has by the late revisers been sufficiently shown. The faults of all are indeed numerous and gross, and have not only corrupted many passages perhaps beyond recovery, but have brought others into suspicion, which are only obscured by obsolete phraseology, or by the writer's unskilfulness and affectation. To alter is more easy than to explain, and temerity is a more common quality than diligence. Those who saw that they must employ conjecture to a certain degree, were willing to indulge it a little further. Had the authour published his own works, we should have sat quietly down to disentangle his intricacies, and clear his obscurities; but now we tear what we cannot loose, and eject what we happen not to understand.

The faults are more than could have happened without the concurrence of many causes. The stile of *Shakespeare* was in itself ungrammatical, perplexed and obscure; his works were transcribed for the players by those who may be supposed to have seldom understood them; they were transmitted by copiers equally unskilful, who still multiplied errours; they were perhaps sometimes mutilated by the actors, for the sake of shortening the speeches ; and were at last printed without correction of the press.

In this state they remained, not as Dr. *Warburton* supposes, because they were unregarded, but because the editor's art was not yet applied to modern languages, and our ancestors were accustomed to so much negligence of *English* printers, that they could very patiently endure it. At last an edition was undertaken by *Rowe* ; not because a poet was to be published by a poet, for *Rowe* seems to have thought very little on correction or explanation, but that our authour's works might appear like those of his fraternity, with the appendages of a life and recommendatory preface. *Rowe* has been clamorously blamed for not performing what he did not undertake, and it is time that justice be done him, by confessing, that though he seems to have had no thought of corruption beyond the printer's errours, yet he has made many emendations, if they were not made before, which his successors have received without acknowledgement, and which, if they had produced them, would have filled pages and pages with censures of the stupidity by which the faults were committed, with displays of the absurdities which they involved, with ostentatious expositions of the new reading, and self congratulations on the happiness of discovering it.

Of *Rowe*, as of all the editors, I have preserved the preface, and have likewise retained the authour's life, though not written with much elegance or spirit ; it relates however what is now to be known, and therefore deserves to pass through all succeeding publications.

The nation had been for many years content enough with Mr. *Rowe*'s performance, when Mr. *Pope* made them acquainted with the true state of *Shakespeare*'s text, shewed that it was extremely corrupt, and gave reason to hope that there were means of reforming it. He collated the old copies, which none had thought to examine before, and restored many lines to their integrity ; but, by a very compendious criticism, he rejected whatever he disliked, and thought more of amputation than of cure.

I know not why he is commended by Dr. *Warburton* for distinguishing the genuine from the spurious plays. In this choice he exerted no judgement of his own ; the plays which he received, were given by *Hemings* and *Condel*, the first editors ; and those which he rejected, though, according to the licentiousness of the press in those times, they were printed during *Shakespeare*'s life, with his name, had been omitted by his friends, and were never added to his works before the edition of 1664, from which they were copied by the later printers.

This was a work which *Pope* seems to have thought unworthy of his abilities, being not able to suppress his contempt of *the dull duty of an editor*. He understood but half his undertaking. The duty of a collator is indeed dull, yet, like other tedious tasks, is very necessary ; but an emendatory critick would ill discharge his duty, without qualities very different from dullness. In perusing a corrupted piece, he must have before him all possibilities of meaning, with all possibilities of expression. Such must be his comprehension of thought, and such his copiousness of language. Out of many readings possible, he must be able to select that which best suits with the state of opinions, and modes of language prevailing in every age, and with his authour's particular cast of thought, and turn of expression. Such must be his knowledge, and such his taste. Conjectural criticism demands more than humanity possesses, and he that exercises it with most praise has very frequent need of indulgence. Let us now be told no more of the dull duty of an editor.

Confidence is the common consequence of success. They whose excellence of any kind has been loudly celebrated, are ready to conclude, that their powers are universal. *Pope*'s edition fell below his own expectations, and he was so much offended, when he was found to have left any thing for others to do, that he past the latter part of his life in a state of hostility with verbal criticism.

I have retained all his notes, that no fragment of so great a writer may be lost; his preface, valuable alike for elegance of composition and justness of remark, and containing a general criticism on his authour, so extensive that little can be added, and so exact, that little can be disputed, every editor has an interest to suppress, but that every reader would demand its insertion.

Pope was succeeded by *Theobald*, a man of narrow comprehension and small acquisitions, with no native and intrinsick splendour of genius, with little of the artificial light of learning, but zealous for minute accuracy, and not negligent in pursuing it. He collated the ancient copies, and rectified many errors. A man so anxiously scrupulous might have been expected to do more, but what little he did was commonly right.

In his report of copies and editions he is not to be trusted, without examination. He speaks sometimes indefinitely of copies, when he has only one. In his enumeration of editions, he mentions the two first folios as of high, and the third folio as of middle authority; but the truth is, that the first is equivalent to all others, and that the rest only deviate from it by the printer's negligence. Whoever has any of the folios has all, excepting those diversities which mere reiteration of editions will produce. I collated them all at the beginning, but afterwards used only the first.

Of his notes I have generally retained those which he retained himself in his second edition, except when they were confuted by subsequent annotators, or were too minute to merit preservation. I have sometimes adopted his restoration of a comma, without inserting the panegyrick in which he celebrated himself for his atchievement. The exuberant excrescence of his diction I have often lopped, his triumphant exultations over *Pope* and *Rowe* I have sometimes suppressed, and his contemptible ostentation I have frequently concealed; but I have in some places shewn him, as he would have shewn himself, for the reader's diversion, that the inflated emptiness of some notes may justify or excuse the contraction of the rest.

Theobald, thus weak and ignorant, thus mean and faithless, thus petulant and ostentatious, by the good luck of having *Pope* for his enemy, has escaped, and escaped alone, with reputation, from this undertaking. So willingly does the world support those who solicite favour, against those who command reverence; and so easily is he praised, whom no man can envy.

Our authour fell then into the hands of Sir *Thomas Hanmer*, the *Oxford* editor, a man, in my opinion, eminently qualified by nature for such studies. He had, what is the first requisite to emendatory criticism, that intuition by which the poet's intention is immediately discovered, and that dexterity of intellect which despatches its work by the easiest means. He had undoubtedly read much; his acquaintance with customs, opinions, and traditions, seems to have been large; and he is often learned without shew. He seldom passes what he does not understand, without an attempt to find or to make a meaning, and sometimes hastily makes what a little more attention would have found. He is solicitous to reduce to grammar, what he could not be sure that his authour intended to be grammatical. *Shakespeare* regarded more the series of ideas, than of words ; and his language, not being designed for the reader's desk, was all that he desired it to be, if it conveyed his meaning to the audience.

Hanmer's care of the metre has been too violently censured. He found the measures reformed in so many passages, by the silent labours of some editors, with the silent acquiescence of the rest, that he thought himself allowed to extend a little further the license, which had already been carried so far without reprehension ; and of his corrections in general, it must be confessed, that they are often just, and made commonly with the least possible violation of the text.

But, by inserting his emendations, whether invented or borrowed, into the page, without any notice of varying copies, he has appropriated the labour of his predecessors, and made his own edition of little authority. His confidence indeed, both in himself and others, was too great ; he supposes all to be right that was done by *Pope* and *Theobald* ; he seems not to suspect a critick of fallibility, and it was but reasonable that he should claim what he so liberally granted.

As he never writes without careful enquiry and diligent consideration, I have received all his notes, and believe that every reader will wish for more.

Of the last editor it is more difficult to speak. Respect is due to high place, tenderness to living reputation, and veneration to genius and learning ; but he cannot be justly offended at that liberty of which he has himself so frequently given an example, nor very solicitous what is thought of notes, which he ought never to have considered as part of his serious employments, and which, I suppose, since the ardour of composition is remitted, he no longer numbers among his happy effusions.

The original and predominant errour of his commentary, is acquiescence in his first thoughts ; that precipitation which is produced by consciousness of quick discernment ; and that confidence which presumes to do, by surveying the surface, what labour only can perform, by penetrating the bottom. His notes exhibit sometimes perverse interpretations, and sometimes improbable conjectures ; he at one time gives the authour more profundity of meaning, than the sentence admits, and at another discovers absurdities, where the sense is plain to every other reader. But his emendations are likewise often happy and just ; and his interpretation of obscure passages learned and sagacious.

Of his notes, I have commonly rejected those, against which the general voice of the publick has exclaimed, or which their own incongruity immediately condemns, and which, I suppose, the authour himself would desire to be forgotten. Of the rest, to part I have given the highest approbation, by inserting the offered reading in the text ; part I have left to the judgment of the reader, as doubtful, though specious ; and part I have censured without reserve, but I am sure without bitterness of malice, and, I hope, without wantonness of insult.

It is no pleasure to me, in revising my volumes, to observe how much paper is wasted in confutation. Whoever considers the revolutions of learning, and the various questions of greater or less importance, upon which wit and reason have exercised their powers, must lament the unsuccessfulness of enquiry, and the slow advances of truth, when he reflects, that great part of the labour of every writer is only the destruction of those that went before him. The first care

of the builder of a new system, is to demolish the
fabricks which are standing. The chief desire of him
that comments an authour, is to shew how much
other commentators have corrupted and obscured
him. The opinions prevalent in one age, as truths
above the reach of controversy, are confuted and
rejected in another, and rise again to reception in
remoter times. Thus the human mind is kept in
motion without progress. Thus sometimes truth and
errour, and sometimes contrarieties of errour, take
each other's place by reciprocal invasion. The tide of
seeming knowledge which is poured over one generation, retires and leaves another naked and barren ;
the sudden meteors of intelligence which for a while
appear to shoot their beams into the regions of
obscurity, on a sudden withdraw their lustre, and
leave mortals again to grope their way.

These elevations and depressions of renown, and
the contradictions to which all improvers of knowledge
must for ever be exposed, since they are not escaped
by the highest and brightest of mankind, may surely
be endured with patience by criticks and annotators,
who can rank themselves but as the satellites of their
authours. How canst thou beg for life, says *Achilles*
to his captive, when thou knowest that thou art now
to suffer only what must another day be suffered by
Achilles?

Dr. *Warburton* had a name sufficient to confer
celebrity on those who could exalt themselves into
antagonists, and his notes have raised a clamour too
loud to be distinct. His chief assailants are the
authours of *the Canons of criticism* and of the *Review
of* Shakespeare's *text* ; of whom one ridicules his
errours with airy petulance, suitable enough to the
levity of the controversy ; the other attacks them
with gloomy malignity, as if he were dragging to

justice an assassin or incendiary. The one stings like a fly, sucks a little blood, takes a gay flutter, and returns for more ; the other bites like a viper, and would be glad to leave inflammations and gangrene behind him. When I think on one, with his confederates, I remember the danger of *Coriolanus*, who was afraid that *girls with spits, and boys with stones, should slay him in puny battle* ; when the other crosses my imagination, I remember the prodigy in *Macbeth*,

> *An eagle tow'ring in his pride of place,*
> *Was by a mousing owl hawk'd at and kill'd.*

Let me however do them justice. One is a wit, and one a scholar. They have both shown acuteness sufficient in the discovery of faults, and have both advanced some probable interpretations of obscure passages ; but when they aspire to conjecture and emendation, it appears how falsely we all estimate our own abilities, and the little which they have been able to perform might have taught them more candour to the endeavours of others.

Before Dr. *Warburton*'s edition, *Critical observations on* Shakespeare had been published by Mr. *Upton*, a man skilled in languages, and acquainted with books, but who seems to have had no great vigour of genius or nicety of taste. Many of his explanations are curious and useful, but he likewise, though he professed to oppose the licentious confidence of editors, and adhere to the old copies, is unable to restrain the rage of emendation, though his ardour is ill seconded by his skill. Every cold empirick, when his heart is expanded by a successful experiment, swells into a theorist, and the laborious collator at some unlucky moment frolicks in conjecture.

Critical, historical and explanatory notes have been likewise published upon *Shakespeare* by Dr. *Grey*,

whose diligent perusal of the old *English* writers has
enabled him to make some useful observations. What
he undertook he has well enough performed, but as
he neither attempts judicial nor emendatory criticism,
he employs rather his memory than his sagacity. It
were to be wished that all would endeavour to imitate
his modesty who have not been able to surpass his
knowledge.

I can say with great sincerity of all my predecessors,
what I hope will hereafter be said of me, that not one
has left *Shakespeare* without improvement, nor is there
one to whom I have not been indebted for assistance
and information. Whatever I have taken from them
it was my intention to refer to its original authour,
and it is certain, that what I have not given to another,
I believed when I wrote it to be my own. In some
perhaps I have been anticipated; but if I am ever
found to encroach upon the remarks of any other
commentator, I am willing that the honour, be it more
or less, should be transferred to the first claimant, for
his right, and his alone, stands above dispute; the
second can prove his pretensions only to himself, nor
can himself always distinguish invention, with sufficient
certainty, from recollection.

They have all been treated by me with candour,
which they have not been careful of observing to one
another. It is not easy to discover from what cause
the acrimony of a scholiast can naturally proceed.
The subjects to be discussed by him are of very
small importance; they involve neither property
nor liberty; nor favour the interest of sect or party.
The various readings of copies, and different interpretations of a passage, seem to be questions that
might exercise the wit, without engaging the passions.
But, whether it be, that *small things make mean men
proud*, and vanity catches small occasions; or that all

contrariety of opinion, even in those that can defend
it no longer, makes proud men angry ; there is often
found in commentaries a spontaneous strain of invective and contempt, more eager and venomous than
is vented by the most furious controvertist in politicks
against those whom he is hired to defame.

Perhaps the lightness of the matter may conduce
to the vehemence of the agency ; when the truth to
be investigated is so near to inexistence, as to escape
attention, its bulk is to be enlarged by rage and
exclamation : That to which all would be indifferent
in its original state, may attract notice when the fate
of a name is appended to it. A commentator has
indeed great temptations to supply by turbulence
what he wants of dignity, to beat his little gold to
a spacious surface, to work that to foam which no art
or diligence can exalt to spirit.

The notes which I have borrowed or written are
either illustrative, by which difficulties are explained ;
or judicial, by which faults and beauties are remarked ;
or emendatory, by which depravations are corrected.

The explanations transcribed from others, if I do
not subjoin any other interpretation, I suppose commonly to be right, at least I intend by acquiescence
to confess, that I have nothing better to propose.

After the labours of all the editors, I found many
passages which appeared to me likely to obstruct the
greater number of readers, and thought it my duty
to facilitate their passage. It is impossible for an
expositor not to write too little for some, and too
much for others. He can only judge what is necessary
by his own experience ; and how long soever he may
deliberate, will at last explain many lines which the
learned will think impossible to be mistaken, and omit
many for which the ignorant will want his help. These
are censures merely relative, and must be quietly

endured. I have endeavoured to be neither super-fluously copious, nor scrupulously reserved, and hope that I have made my authour's meaning accessible to many who before were frighted from perusing him, and contributed something to the publick, by diffusing innocent and rational pleasure.

The compleat explanation of an authour not systematick and consequential, but desultory and vagrant, abounding in casual allusions and light hints, is not to be expected from any single scholiast. All personal reflections, when names are suppressed, must be in a few years irrecoverably obliterated; and cus-toms, too minute to attract the notiçe of law, such as modes of dress, formalities of conversation, rules of visits, disposition of furniture, and practices of cere-mony, which naturally find places in familiar dialogue, are so fugitive and unsubstantial, that they are not easily retained or recovered. What can be known, will be collected by chance, from the recesses of obscure and obsolete papers, perused commonly with some other view. Of this knowledge every man has some, and none has much ; but when an authour has engaged the publick attention, those who can add any thing to his illustration, communicate their discoveries, and time produces what had eluded diligence.

To time I have been obliged to resign many passages, which, though I did not understand them, will perhaps hereafter be explained, having, I hope, illustrated some, which others have neglected or mistaken, some-times by short remarks, or marginal directions, such as every editor has added at his will, and often by comments more laborious than the matter will seem to deserve ; but that which is most difficult is not always most important, and to an editor nothing is a trifle by which his authour is obscured.

The poetical beauties or defects I have not been

very diligent to observe. Some plays have more, and some fewer judicial observations, not in proportion to their difference of merit, but because I gave this part of my design to chance and to caprice. The reader, I believe, is seldom pleased to find his opinion anticipated; it is natural to delight more in what we find or make, than in what we receive. Judgement, like other faculties, is improved by practice, and its advancement is hindered by submission to dictatorial decisions, as the memory grows torpid by the use of a table book. Some initiation is however necessary; of all skill, part is infused by precept, and part is obtained by habit; I have therefore shewn so much as may enable the candidate of criticism to discover the rest.

To the end of most plays, I have added short strictures, containing a general censure of faults, or praise of excellence; in which I know not how much I have concurred with the current opinion; but I have not, by any affectation of singularity, deviated from it. Nothing is minutely and particularly examined, and therefore it is to be supposed, that in the plays which are condemned there is much to be praised, and in those which are praised much to be condemned.

The part of criticism in which the whole succession of editors has laboured with the greatest diligence, which has occasioned the most arrogant ostentation, and excited the keenest acrimony, is the emendation of corrupted passages, to which the publick attention having been first drawn by the violence of contention between *Pope* and *Theobald*, has been continued by the persecution, which, with a kind of conspiracy, has been since raised against all the publishers of *Shakespeare*.

That many passages have passed in a state of depravation through all the editions is indubitably certain;

of these the restoration is only to be attempted by collation of copies or sagacity of conjecture. The collator's province is safe and easy, the conjecturer's perilous and difficult. Yet as the greater part of the plays are extant only in one copy, the peril must not be avoided, nor the difficulty refused.

Of the readings which this emulation of amendment has hitherto produced, some from the labours of every publisher I have advanced into the text; those are to be considered as in my opinion sufficiently supported; some I have rejected without mention, as evidently erroneous; some I have left in the notes without censure or approbation, as resting in equipoise between objection and defence; and some, which seemed specious but not right, I have inserted with a subsequent animadversion.

Having classed the observations of others, I was at last to try what I could substitute for their mistakes, and how I could supply their omissions. I collated such copies as I could procure, and wished for more, but have not found the collectors of these rarities very communicative. Of the editions which chance or kindness put into my hands I have given an enumeration, that I may not be blamed for neglecting what I had not the power to do.

By examining the old copies, I soon found that the later publishers, with all their boasts of diligence, suffered many passages to stand unauthorised, and contented themselves with *Rowe*'s regulation of the text, even where they knew it to be arbitrary, and with a little consideration might have found it to be wrong. Some of these alterations are only the ejection of a word for one that appeared to him more elegant or more intelligible. These corruptions I have often silently rectified; for the history of our language, and the true force of our words, can only be preserved, by keeping the text of authours free from adulteration. Others, and those very frequent, smoothed the cadence, or regulated the measure ; on these I have not exercised the same rigour ; if only a word was transposed, or a particle inserted or omitted, I have sometimes suffered the line to stand ; for the inconstancy of the copies is such, as that some liberties may be easily permitted. But this practice I have not suffered to proceed far, having restored the primitive diction wherever it could for any reason be preferred.

The emendations, which comparison of copies supplied, I have inserted in the text ; sometimes where the improvement was slight, without notice, and sometimes with an account of the reasons of the change.

Conjecture, though it be sometimes unavoidable, I have not wantonly nor licentiously indulged. It has been my settled principle, that the reading of the ancient books is probably true, and therefore is not to be disturbed for the sake of elegance, perspicuity, or mere improvement of the sense. For though much credit is not due to the fidelity, nor any to the judgement of the first publishers, yet they who had the copy before their eyes were more likely to read it right, than we who read it only by imagination. But it is evident that they have often made strange mistakes by ignorance or negligence, and that therefore something may be properly attempted by criticism, keeping the middle way between presumption and timidity.

Such criticism I have attempted to practise, and where any passage appeared inextricably perplexed, have endeavoured to discover how it may be recalled to sense, with least violence. But my first labour is, always to turn the old text on every side, and try if there be any interstice, through which light can find its way ; nor would *Huetius* himself condemn me, as refusing the trouble of research, for the ambition of alteration. In this modest industry I have not been unsuccessful. I have rescued many lines from the violations of temerity, and secured many scenes from the inroads of correction. I have adopted the *Roman* sentiment, that it is more honourable to save a citizen, than to kill an enemy, and have been more careful to protect than to attack.

I have preserved the common distribution of the plays into acts, though I believe it to be in almost all the plays void of authority. Some of those which are divided in the later editions have no division in the first folio, and some that are divided in the folio have no division in the preceding copies. The settled mode of the theatre requires four intervals in the play, but few, if any, of our authour's compositions can be properly distributed in that manner. An act is so much of the drama as passes without intervention of time or change of place. A pause makes a new act. In every real, and therefore in every imitative action, the intervals may be more or fewer, the restriction of five acts being accidental and arbitrary. This *Shakespeare* knew, and this he practised; his plays were written, and at first printed in one unbroken continuity, and ought now to be exhibited with short pauses, interposed as often as the scene is changed, or any considerable time is required to pass. This method would at once quell a thousand absurdities.

In restoring the authour's works to their integrity, I have considered the punctuation as wholly in my power; for what could be their care of colons and commas, who corrupted words and sentences. Whatever could be done by adjusting points is therefore silently performed, in some plays with much diligence, in others with less; it is hard to keep a busy eye steadily fixed upon evanescent atoms, or a discursive mind upon evanescent truth.

The same liberty has been taken with a few particles, or other words of slight effect. I have sometimes inserted or omitted them without notice. I have done that sometimes, which the other editors have done always, and which indeed the state of the text may sufficiently justify.

The greater part of readers, instead of blaming us for passing trifles, will wonder that on mere trifles so much labour is expended, with such importance of debate, and such solemnity of diction. To these I answer with confidence, that they are judging of an art which they do not understand; yet cannot much reproach them with their ignorance, nor promise that they would become in general, by learning criticism, more useful, happier or wiser.

As I practised conjecture more, I learned to trust it less; and after I had printed a few plays, resolved to insert none of my own readings in the text. Upon this caution I now congratulate myself, for every day encreases my doubt of my emendations.

Since I have confined my imagination to the margin, it must not be considered as very reprehensible, if I have suffered it to play some freaks in its own dominion. There is no danger in conjecture, if it be proposed as conjecture; and while the text remains uninjured, those changes may be safely offered, which are not considered even by him that offers them as necessary or safe.

If my readings are of little value, they have not been ostentatiously displayed or importunately obtruded. I could have written longer notes, for the art of writing notes is not of difficult attainment. The work is performed, first by railing at the stupidity, negligence, ignorance, and asinine tastelessness of the former editors, and shewing, from all that goes before and all that follows, the inelegance and absurdity of the old reading; then by proposing something, which to superficial readers would seem specious, but which the editor rejects with indignation; then by producing the true reading, with a long paraphrase, and concluding with loud acclamations on the discovery, and a sober wish for the advancement and prosperity of genuine criticism.

All this may be done, and perhaps done sometimes without impropriety. But I have always suspected that the reading is right, which requires many words to prove it wrong; and the emendation wrong, that cannot without so much labour appear to be right. The justness of a happy restoration strikes at once, and the moral precept may be well applied to criticism, *quod dubitas ne feceris.*

To dread the shore which he sees spread with wrecks, is natural to the sailor. I had before my eye, so many critical adventures ended in miscarriage, that caution was forced upon me. I encountered in every page Wit struggling with its own sophistry, and Learning confused by the multiplicity of its views. I was forced to censure those whom I admired, and could not but reflect, while I was dispossessing their emendations, how soon the same fate might happen to my own, and how many of the readings which I have corrected may be by some other editor defended and established.

> *Criticks, I saw, that other's names efface,*
> *And fix their own, with labour, in the place;*
> *Their own, like others, soon their place resign'd,*
> *Or disappear'd, and left the first behind.* POPE.

That a conjectural critick should often be mistaken, cannot be wonderful, either to others or himself, if it be considered, that in his art there is no system, no principal and axiomatical truth that regulates subordinate positions. His chance of errour is re-

newed at every attempt; an oblique view of the
passage, a slight misapprehension of a phrase, a casual
inattention to the parts connected, is sufficient to
make him not only fail, but fail ridiculously; and
when he succeeds best, he produces perhaps but one
reading of many probable, and he that suggests another
will always be able to dispute his claims.

It is an unhappy state, in which danger is hid under
pleasure. The allurements of emendation are scarcely
resistible. Conjecture has all the joy and all the pride
of invention, and he that has once started a happy
change, is too much delighted to consider what objections may rise against it.

Yet conjectural criticism has been of great use in the
learned world; nor is it my intention to depreciate
a study, that has exercised so many mighty minds,
from the revival of learning to our own age, from the
Bishop of *Aleria* to English *Bentley*. The criticks on
ancient authours have, in the exercise of their sagacity,
many assistances, which the editor of *Shakespeare* is
condemned to want. They are employed upon grammatical and settled languages, whose construction contributes so much to perspicuity, that *Homer* has fewer
passages unintelligible than *Chaucer*. The words have
not only a known regimen, but invariable quantities,
which direct and confine the choice. There are commonly more manuscripts than one; and they do not
often conspire in the same mistakes. Yet *Scaliger*
could confess to *Salmasius* how little satisfaction his
emendations gave him. *Illudunt nobis conjecturæ no-
stræ, quarum nos pudet, posteaquam in meliores codices
incidimus.* And *Lipsius* could complain, that criticks
were making faults, by trying to remove them, *Ut
olim vitiis, ita nunc remediis laboratur.* And indeed,
where mere conjecture is to be used, the emendations
of *Scaliger* and *Lipsius*, notwithstanding their wonder-

ful sagacity and erudition, are often vague and disputable, like mine or *Theobald*'s.

Perhaps I may not be more censured for doing wrong, than for doing little ; for raising in the publick expectations, which at last I have not answered. The expectation of ignorance is indefinite, and that of knowledge is often tyrannical. It is hard to satisfy those who know not what to demand, or those who demand by design what they think impossible to be done. I have indeed disappointed no opinion more than my own ; yet I have endeavoured to perform my task with no slight solicitude. Not a single passage in the whole work has appeared to me corrupt, which I have not attempted to restore ; or obscure, which I have not endeavoured to illustrate. In many I have failed like others ; and from many, after all my efforts, I have retreated, and confessed the repulse. I have not passed over, with affected superiority, what is equally difficult to the reader and to myself, but where I could not instruct him, have owned my ignorance. I might easily have accumulated a mass of seeming learning upon easy scenes ; but it ought not to be imputed to negligence, that, where nothing was necessary, nothing has been done, or that, where others have said enough, I have said no more.

Notes are often necessary, but they are necessary evils. Let him, that is yet unacquainted with the powers of *Shakespeare*, and who desires to feel the highest pleasure that the drama can give, read every play from the first scene to the last, with utter negligence of all his commentators. When his fancy is once on the wing, let it not stoop at correction or explanation. When his attention is strongly engaged, let it disdain alike to turn aside to the name of *Theobald* and of *Pope*. Let him read on through brightness and obscurity, through integrity and corruption ; let him preserve his comprehension of the dialogue and his interest in the fable. And when the pleasures of novelty have ceased, let him attempt exactness, and read the commentators.

Particular passages are cleared by notes, but the general effect of the work is weakened. The mind is refrigerated by interruption; the thoughts are diverted from the principal subject; the reader is weary, he suspects not why; and at last throws away the book, which he has too diligently studied.

Parts are not to be examined till the whole has been surveyed; there is a kind of intellectual remoteness necessary for the comprehension of any great work in its full design and its true proportions; a close approach shews the smaller niceties, but the beauty of the whole is discerned no longer.

It is not very grateful to consider how little the succession of editors has added to this authour's power of pleasing. He was read, admired, studied, and imitated, while he was yet deformed with all the improprieties which ignorance and neglect could accumulate upon him; while the reading was yet not rectified, nor his allusions understood; yet then did *Dryden* pronounce " that *Shakespeare* was the man, who, of all modern and perhaps ancient poets, had the largest and most comprehensive soul. All the images of nature were still present to him, and he drew them not laboriously, but luckily: When he describes any thing, you more than see it, you feel it too. Those who accuse him to have wanted learning, give him the greater commendation: he was naturally learned: he needed not the spectacles of books to read nature; he looked inwards, and found her there. I cannot say he is every where alike; were he so, I should do him injury to compare him with the greatest of mankind. He is many times flat and

insipid; his comick wit degenerating into clenches,
his serious swelling into bombast. But he is always
great, when some great occasion is presented to him:
No man can say, he ever had a fit subject for his wit,
and did not then raise himself as high above the rest
of poets,

Quantum lenta solent inter viburna cupressi."

It is to be lamented, that such a writer should want
a commentary; that his language should become
obsolete, or his sentiments obscure. But it is vain
to carry wishes beyond the condition of human things;
that which must happen to all, has happened to
Shakespeare, by accident and time; and more than
has been suffered by any other writer since the use of
types, has been suffered by him through his own
negligence of fame, or perhaps by that superiority of
mind, which despised its own performances, when it
compared them with its powers, and judged those
works unworthy to be preserved, which the criticks of
following ages were to contend for the fame of restoring
and explaining.

Among these candidates of inferiour fame, I am now
to stand the judgment of the publick; and wish that
I could confidently produce my commentary as equal
to the encouragement which I have had the honour
of receiving. Every work of this kind is by its nature
deficient, and I should feel little solicitude about the
sentence, were it to be pronounced only by the skilful
and the learned.

NOTES ON THE PLAYS

THE TEMPEST.

THESE two first Plays, the *Tempest* and the *Midsummer-night's Dream*, are the noblest Efforts of that sublime and amazing Imagination, peculiar to *Shakespeare*, which soars above the Bounds of Nature without forsaking Sense : or, more properly, carries Nature along with him beyond her established Limits. *Fletcher* seems particularly to have admired these two Plays, and hath wrote two in Imitation of them, the *Sea-Voyage* and the *Faithful Shepherdess*. But when he presumes to break a Lance with *Shakespeare*, and write in emulation of him, as he does in the *False one*, which is the Rival of *Anthony* and *Cleopatra*, he is not so successful. After him, Sir *John Suckling* and *Milton* catched the brightest Fire of their Imagination from these two Plays ; which shines fantastically indeed, in the *Goblins*, but much more nobly and serenely in *The Mask at Ludlow-Castle*.— WARBURTON.

ACT I. SCENE i.

It may be observed of *Gonzalo*, that, being the only good Man that appears with the King, he is the only Man that preserves his Cheerfulness in the Wreck, and his Hope on the Island.

ACT I. SCENE iii. (I. ii.)

That the Character and Conduct of *Prospero* may be understood, something must be known of the System of Enchantment, which supplied all the Marvellous found in the Romances of the middle Ages. This system seems to be founded on the Opinion that the fallen Spirits, having different Degrees of Guilt, had different Habitations alloted them at their Expulsion, some being confined in Hell, *some*, as

Hooker, who delivers the Opinion of our Poet's Age, expresses it, *dispersed in Air, some on Earth, some in Water, others in Caves, Dens or Minerals under the Earth.* Of these some were more malignant and mischievous than others. The earthy Spirits seem to have been thought the most depraved, and the aerial the least vitiated. Thus *Prospero* observes of *Ariel,*

—— *Thou wast a Spirit too delicate*
To act her earthy *and abhorred Commands.*

Over these Spirits a Power might be obtained by certain Rites performed or Charms learned. This Power was called the *Black Art,* or *Knowledge of Enchantment.* The Enchanter being, as King *James* observes in his *Demonology,* one *who commands the Devil, whereas the Witch serves him.* Those who thought best of this Art, the Existence of which was, I am afraid, believed very seriously, held that certain Sounds and Characters had a physical Power over Spirits, and compelled their Agency; others who condemned the Practice, which in reality was surely never practised, were of Opinion, with more Reason, that the Power of Charms arose *only* from compact, and was no more than the Spirits voluntary allowed them for the Seduction of Man. The Art was held by all, though not equally criminal yet unlawful, and therefore *Casaubon,* speaking of one who had Commerce with Spirits, blames him, though he imagines him *one of the best Kind who dealt with them by Way of Command.* Thus *Prospero* repents of his Art in the last Scene. The Spirits were always considered as in some Measure enslaved to the Enchanter, at least for a Time, and as serving with Unwillingness, therefore *Ariel* so often begs for Liberty; and *Caliban* observes that the Spirits serve *Prospero* with no good Will, but *hate him rootedly.* —Of these Trifles enough.

ACT I. SCENE iv.

> It was a tradition, it seems, that Lord *Falkland*, Lord *C. J. Vaughan*, and Mr. *Seldon* concurred in observing, that *Shakespear* had not only found out a new character in his *Caliban*, but had also devised and adapted a *new manner of language* for that character.—WARBURTON.

Whence these criticks derived the notion of a new language appropriated to *Caliban* I cannot find: They certainly mistook brutality of sentiment for uncouthness of words. *Caliban* had learned to speak of *Prospero* and his daughter, he had no names for the sun and moon before their arrival, and could not have invented a language of his own without more understanding than *Shakespear* has thought it proper to bestow upon him. His diction is indeed somewhat clouded by the gloominess of his temper and the malignity of his purposes; but let any other being entertain the same thoughts and he will find them easily issue in the same expressions.

ACT I. SCENE v. (I. ii. 375, 394.)

> On Ariel's songs: *Come unto these yellow sands*,
>   and *Full fathom five thy father lies.*

I know not whether Dr. *Warburton* has very successfully defended these Songs from *Gildon's* accusation. *Ariel's* lays, however seasonable and efficacious, must be allowed to be of no supernatural dignity or elegance, they express nothing great, nor reveal any thing above mortal discovery.

The reason for which *Ariel* is introduced thus trifling is, that he and his companions are evidently of the fairy kind, an order of Beings to which tradition has always ascribed a sort of diminutive agency, powerful but ludicrous, a humorous and frolick controlment of nature, well expressed by the Songs of *Ariel*.

A MIDSUMMER-NIGHT'S DREAM.

ACT I. SCENE iv.

IN this Scene *Shakespeare* takes advantage of his knowledge of the theatre, to ridicule the prejudices and competitions of the Players. *Bottom*, who is generally acknowledged the principal Actor, declares his inclination to be for a tyrant, for a part of fury, tumult, and noise, such as every young man pants to perform when he first steps upon the Stage. The same *Bottom*, who seems bred in a tiring-room, has another histrionical passion. He is for engrossing every part, and would exclude his inferiors from all possibility of distinction. He is therefore desirous to play *Pyramus*, *Thisbe* and the *Lyon* at the same time.

ACT I. SCENE iv. (I. ii. 50–3).

FLUTE. *Nay, faith, let me not play a woman; I have a beard coming.*

QUINCE. *That's all one; you shall play it in a masque.*

This passage shews how the want of women on the old Stage was supplied. If they had not a young man who could perform the part with a face that might pass for feminine, the character was acted in a mask, which was at that time a part of a Lady's dress so much in use that it did not give any unusual appearance to the Scene; and he that could modulate his voice in a female tone might play the woman very successfully. It is observed in *Downes's* Memoirs of the Playhouse, that one of these counterfeit heroines moved the passions more strongly than the women that have since been brought upon the stage. Some of the catastrophes of the old comedies, which make Lovers marry the wrong women, are, by recollection of the common use of masks, brought nearer to probability.

ACT I. SCENE iv. (I. ii. 96–9.)

BOTTOM. *I will discharge it in either your straw-colour'd beard,*
your orange-tawny beard, your purple-in-grain beard, or your
French crown-colour'd beard; your perfect yellow.

Here *Bottom* again discovers a true genius for the
Stage by his solicitude for propriety of dress, and his
deliberation which beard to chuse among many beards,
all unnatural.

ACT II. SCENE i. (II. i. 42–57.) *Puck.*

A like account of *Puck* is given by *Drayton,*

> *He meeteth* Puck, *which most men call*
> Hobgoblin, *and on him doth fall.——*
> *This* Puck *seems but a dreaming dolt,*
> *Still walking like a ragged colt,*
> *And oft out of a bush doth bolt,*
> *Of purpose to deceive us;*
> *And leading us makes us to stray,*
> *Long winter's nights out of the way,*
> *And when we stick in mire and clay,*
> *He doth with laughter leave us.*

It will be apparent to him that shall compare *Dray-*
ton's Poem with this play, that either one of the poets
copied the other, or, as I rather believe, that there was
then some system of the fairy empire generally received,
which they both represented as accurately as they could.
Whether *Drayton* or *Shakespeare* wrote first, I cannot
discover.

ACT II. SCENE ii. (II. i. 82–114.)

And never since the middle Summer's spring, &c.

There are not many passages in *Shakespear* which
one can be certain he has borrowed from the Ancients;
but this is one of the few that, I think, will admit of
no dispute. Our Author's admirable description of
the miseries of the Country being plainly an imitation

of that which *Ovid* draws, as consequent on the grief of *Ceres*, for the loss of her daughter.

> *Nescit adhuc ubi sit : terras tamen increpat omnes :*
> *Ingratasque vocat, nec frugum munere dignas.*
> ————*Ergo illic sæva vertentia glebas*
> Fregit aratra manu *parilique irata colonos*
> *Ruricolasque boves letho dedit : arvaque jussit*
> Fallere depositum vitiataque semina fecit.
> *Fertilitas terræ latum vulgata per orbem*
> *Sparsa jacet.* Primis segetes moriuntur in herbis.
> *Et modo sol nimius,* nimius modo corripit imber :
> Sideraque ventique nocent.

Act II. Scene ii. (ii. i. 101.)
>   *The human mortals want their winter here.*

After all the endeavours of the Editors this passage still remains to me unintelligible. I cannot see why Winter is, in the general confusion of the year now described, more wanted than any other season. Dr. *Warburton* observes that he alludes to our practice of singing carols in *December* ; but though *Shakespear* is no great chronologer in his dramas, I think he has never so mingled true and false religion, as to give us reason for believing that he would make the moon incensed for the omission of our carols. I therefore imagine him to have meant heathen rites of adoration. This is not all the difficulty. *Titania's* account of this calamity is not sufficiently consequential. *Men find no winter,* therefore they sing no hymns, the moon provoked by this omission alters the seasons. That is, the alteration of the seasons produces the alteration of the seasons. I am far from supposing that *Shakespear* might not sometimes think confusedly, and therefore am not sure that the passage is corrupted. If we should read,

>   *And human mortals want their* wonted year,

Yet will not this licence of alteration much mend the narrative ; the cause and the effect are still confounded. Let us carry critical temerity a little further. *Scaliger* transposed the lines of *Virgil*'s *Gallus*. Why may not the same experiment be ventured upon *Shakespear*.

> *The human mortals want their wonted year,*
> *The seasons alter ; hoary-headed frosts*
> *Fall in the fresh lap of the crimson rose ;*
> *And on old* Hyems' *chin, and icy crown,*
> *An od'rous chaplet of sweet summer buds*
> *Is, as in mock'ry, set. The spring, the summer.*
> *The childing autumn, angry winter, change*
> *Their wonted liveries ; and the 'mazed world,*
> *By their increase, now knows not which is which.*
> *No night is now with hymn or carol blest;*
> *Therefore the moon, the governess of floods,*
> *Pale in her anger, washes all the air;*
> *And thorough this distemperature, we see*
> *That rheumatick diseases do abound.*
> *And this same progeny of evil comes*
> *From our debate, from our dissension.*

I know not what credit the reader will give to this emendation, which I do not much credit myself.

Act III. Scene i.

In the time of *Shakespear* there were many companies of players, sometimes five at the same time, contending for the favour of the publick. Of these some were undoubtedly very unskilful and very poor, and it is probable that the design of this Scene was to ridicule their ignorance, and the odd expedients to which they might be driven by the want of proper decorations. *Bottom* was perhaps the head of a rival house, and is therefore honoured with an Ass's head.

Act III. Scene iii. (III. i. 177.)

> *the fiery glow-worm's eyes.*

I know not how *Shakespeare*, who commonly derived his knowledge of nature from his own observation, happened to place the glow-worm's light in his eyes, which is only in his tail.

Act IV. Scene i. (IV. i. 48–9.)

> *So doth the woodbine the sweet honey-suckle,*
> *Gently entwist.*

Shakespeare perhaps only meant, so the leaves involve the flower, using *woodbine* for the plant and *honey-suckle* for the flower; or perhaps *Shakespeare* made a blunder.

Act IV. Scene i. (IV. i. 110.)

> *Our observation is performed.*

The honours due to the morning of *May*. I know not why *Shakespear* calls this play a *Midsummer-Night's Dream*, when he so carefully informs us that it happened on the night preceding *May* day.

Act V. Scene iii. (V. ii. 31–2.)

> Oberon. *Now until the break of day,*
> *Through this house each* Fairy *stray.*

This speech, which both the old quartos give to *Oberon*, is in the Edition of 1623, and in all the following, printed as the song. I have restored it to *Oberon*, as it apparently contains not the blessing which he intends to bestow on the bed, but his declaration that he will bless it, and his orders to the Fairies how to perform the necessary rites. But where then is the song?—I am afraid it is gone after many other things of greater value. The truth is that two songs are lost. The series of the Scene is this; after the speech of *Puck*, *Oberon* enters, and calls his Fairies to a song, which song is apparently wanting in all the copies. Next *Titania* leads another song which is indeed lost like the former, though the Editors have endeavoured to find it. Then *Oberon* dismisses his Fairies to the despatch of the ceremonies.

The songs, I suppose, were lost, because they were not inserted in the players' parts, from which the drama was printed.

Of this play there are two editions in quarto, one printed for *Thomas Fisher*, the other for *James Roberts*, both in 1600. I have used the copy of *Roberts*, very carefully collated, as it seems, with that of *Fisher*. Neither of the editions approach to exactness. *Fisher* is sometimes preferable, but *Roberts* was followed, though not without some variations, by *Hemings* and *Condel*, and they by all the folios that succeeded them.

Wild and fantastical as it is, all the parts in their various modes are well written, and give the kind of pleasure which the authour designed. Fairies in his time were much in fashion ; common tradition had made them familiar, and *Spenser*'s poem had made them great.

THE TWO GENTLEMEN OF VERONA.

It is observable (I know not for what cause) that the stile of this comedy is less figurative, and more natural and unaffected than the greater part of this author's, tho' supposed to be one of the first he wrote.—POPE.

To this observation of Mr. *Pope*, which is very just, Mr. *Theobald* has added, that this is one of *Shakespear*'s *worst plays, and is less corrupted than any other.* Mr. *Upton* peremptorily determines, *that if any proof can be drawn from manner and style, this play must be sent packing and seek for its parent elsewhere. How otherwise,* says he, *do painters distinguish copies from originals, and have not authours their peculiar style and manner from which a true critick can form as unerring a judgment as a Painter?* I am afraid this illustration of a critick's science will not prove what is desired. A Painter knows a copy from an original by rules somewhat resembling these by which criticks know a translation, which if it be literal, and literal it must be to resemble the copy of a picture, will be easily distinguished. Copies are known from originals even when the painter copies his own picture ; so if an authour should literally translate his work he would lose the manner of an original.

Mr. *Upton* confounds the copy of a picture with the imitation of a painter's manner. Copies are easily known, but good imitations are not detected with equal certainty, and are, by the best judges, often mistaken. Nor is it true that the writer has always peculiarities equally distinguishable with those of the painter. The peculiar manner of each arises from the desire, natural to every performer, of facilitating his subsequent works by recurrence to his former ideas ; this recurrence produces that repetition which is called habit. The painter, whose work is partly intellectual and partly manual, has habits of the mind, the eye and the hand, the writer has only habits of the mind. Yet, some painters have differed as much from themselves as from any other ; and I have been told, that there is little resemblance between the first works of *Raphael* and the last. The same variation may be expected in writers ; and if it be true, as it seems, that they are less subject to habit, the difference between their works may be yet greater.

But by the internal marks of a composition we may discover the authour with probability, though seldom with certainty. When I read this play I cannot but think that I discover both in the serious and ludicrous scenes, the language and sentiments of *Shakespear*. It is not indeed one of his most powerful effusions, it has neither many diversities of character, nor striking delineations of life, but it abounds in γνῶμαι beyond most of his plays, and few have more lines or passages which, singly considered, are eminently beautiful. I am yet inclined to believe that it was not very successful, and suspect that it has escaped corruption, only because being seldom played it was less exposed to the hazards of transcription.

Act I. Scene ii.

That this, like many other Scenes, is mean and vulgar, will be universally allowed; but that it was interpolated by the players seems advanced without any proof, only to give a greater licence to criticism.

Act II. Scene vii. (ii. iv. 137–9.)

> *Love's a mighty lord:*
> *And hath so humbled me as, I confess,*
> *There is no woe to his correction.*

No misery that *can be compared to* the punishment inflicted by love. *Herbert* called for the prayers of the *Liturgy* a little before his death, saying, *None* to *them, none* to *them.*

In this play there is a strange mixture of knowledge and ignorance, of care and negligence. The versification is often excellent, the allusions are learned and just; but the author conveys his heroes by sea from one inland town to another in the same country; he places the Emperour at *Milan* and sends his young men to attend him, but never mentions him more; he makes *Protheus*, after an interview with *Silvia*, say he has only seen her picture, and, if we may credit the old copies, he has by mistaking places, left his scenery

inextricable. The reason of all this confusion seems
to be, that he took his story from a novel which he
sometimes followed, and sometimes forsook, sometimes
remembred, and sometimes forgot.

MEASURE FOR MEASURE.

There is perhaps not one of *Shakespear*'s plays more
darkened than this by the peculiarities of its Authour,
and the unskilfulness of its Editors, by distortions of
phrase, or negligence of transcription.

ACT I. SCENE i. (I. i. 7–9.)

> *Then no more remains ;*
> *But that to your sufficiency, as your worth is able,*
> *And let them work.*

This is a passage which has exercised the sagacity
of the Editors, and is now to employ mine.

Sir *Tho. Hanmer* having caught from Mr. *Theobald*
a hint that a line was lost, endeavours to supply it thus.

> *——Then no more remains,*
> *But that to your sufficiency* you join
> A will to serve us, *as your worth is able.*

He has by this bold conjecture undoubtedly obtained
a meaning, but, perhaps not, even in his own opinion,
the meaning of *Shakespear*.

That the passage is more or less corrupt, I believe
every reader will agree with the Editors. I am not
convinced that a line is lost, as Mr. *Theobald* conjectures, nor that the change of *but* to *put*, which Dr. *Warburton* has admitted after some other Editor, will
amend the fault. There was probably some original
obscurity in the expression, which gave occasion to
mistake in repetition or transcription. I therefore
suspect that the Authour wrote thus,

> ——*Then no more remains,*
> *But that to your* sufficiencies *your worth is* abled,
> *And let them work.*

Then nothing remains more than to tell you that your Virtue is now invested with power equal to your knowledge and wisdom. Let therefore your knowledge and your virtue now work together. It may easily be conceived how *sufficiencies* was, by an inarticulate speaker, or inattentive hearer, confounded with *sufficiency as*, and how *abled*, a word very unusual, was changed into *able*. For *abled*, however, an authority is not wanting. *Lear* uses it in the same sense, or nearly the same, with the Duke. As for *sufficiencies*, D. *Hamilton*, in his dying speech, prays that *Charles* II. *may exceed both the* virtues *and* sufficiencies *of his father*.

Act I. Scene ii. (I. i. 51.)

> *We have with a* leaven'd *and prepared choice.*

Leaven'd has no sense in this place: we should read LEVEL'D *choice.* The allusion is to archery, when a man has fixed upon his object, after taking good aim.—WARBURTON.

No emendation is necessary. *Leaven'd choice* is one of *Shakespear's* harsh metaphors. His train of ideas seems to be this. *I have proceeded to you with choice* mature, concocted, fermented, *leavened*. When Bread is *leavened*, it is left to ferment: a *leavened* choice is therefore a choice not hasty, but considerate, not declared as soon as it fell into the imagination, but suffered to work long in the mind. Thus explained it suits better with *prepared* than *levelled*.

Act II. Scene ix. (II. iii. 11–12.)

> *Who falling in the* flaws *of her own youth,*
> *Hath* blister'd *her report.*

Who does not see that the integrity of the metaphor requires we should read FLAMES *of her own youth.*—WARBURTON.

Who does not see that upon such principles there is no end of correction.

Act III. **Scene** i. (III. i. 13-15.)

> *Thou art not noble:*
> *For all th' accommodations, that thou bear'st,*
> *Are nurs'd by baseness.*

Dr. *Warburton* is undoubtedly mistaken in supposing that by *baseness* is meant *self-love* here assigned as the motive of all human actions. *Shakespear* meant only to observe, that a minute analysis of life at once destroys that splendour which dazzles the imagination. Whatever grandeur can display, or luxury enjoy, is procured by *baseness*, by offices of which the mind shrinks from the contemplation. All the delicacies of the table may be traced back to the shambles and the dunghill, all magnificence of building was hewn from the quarry, and all the pomp of ornaments, dug from among the damps and darkness of the mine.

Act III. **Scene** i. (III. i. 16-17.)

> *The soft and tender fork*
> *Of a poor worm.*

Worm is put for any creeping thing or *serpent*. *Shakespear* supposes falsely, but according to the vulgar notion, that a serpent wounds with his tongue, and that his tongue is *forked*. He confounds reality and fiction, a serpent's tongue is *soft* but not *forked* nor hurtful. If it could hurt, it could not be soft. In *Midsummer-Night's Dream* he has the same notion.

> ———— *With* doubler *tongue*
> *Than thine, O serpent, never adder stung.*

Act III. **Scene** i. (III. i. 17-19.)

> *Thy best of rest is sleep,*
> *And that thou oft provok'st; yet grosly fear'st*
> *Thy death which is no more.*

Evidently from the following passage of *Cicero; Habes somnum imaginem Mortis, eamque quotidie induis, & dubitas quin sensus in morte nullus sit, cum in ejus simulacro videas esse nullum sensum.* But the Epicurean insinuation is, with great judgment, omitted in the imitation.—WARBURTON.

Here Dr. *Warburton* might have found a sentiment worthy of his animadversion. I cannot without indignation find *Shakespear* saying, that *death is only sleep*, lengthening out his exhortation by a sentence which in the *Friar* is impious, in the reasoner is foolish, and in the poet trite and vulgar.

Act III. Scene i. (III. i. 32–4.)

> *Thou hast nor youth, nor age:*
> *But as it were an after dinner's sleep,*
> *Dreaming on both.*

This is exquisitely imagined. When we are young we busy ourselves in forming schemes for succeeding time, and miss the gratifications that are before us; when we are old we amuse the languour of age with the recollection of youthful pleasures or performances; so that our life, of which no part is filled with the business of the present time, resembles our dreams after dinner, when the events of the morning are mingled with the designs of the evening.

Act III. Scene i. (III. i. 36–8.)

> *When thou'rt old and rich,*
> *Thou hast neither heat, affection, limb, nor beauty*
> *To make thy riches pleasant.*

But how does beauty make *riches pleasant?* We should read BOUNTY, which compleats the sense, and is this; Thou hast neither the pleasure of enjoying riches thy self, for thou wantest vigour: nor of seeing it enjoyed by others, for thou wantest *bounty.* Where the making the want of *bounty* as inseparable from old age as the want of *health*, is extremely satirical tho' not altogether just.—WARBURTON.

I am inclined to believe that neither man nor woman will have much difficulty to tell how *beauty makes riches pleasant.* Surely this emendation, though it is elegant and ingenious, is not such as that an opportunity of inserting it should be purchased by declaring ignorance of what every one knows, by confessing insensibility of what every one feels.

ACT III. SCENE ii. (III. i. 137-8.)

> *Is't not a kind of incest, to take life*
> *From thine own sister's shame?*

In *Isabella's* declamation there is something harsh, and something forced and far-fetched. But her indignation cannot be thought violent when we consider her not only as a virgin but as a nun.

ACT IV. SCENE viii. (IV. iii. 4-5.)

> *First here's young Mr.* Rash, &c.

This enumeration of the inhabitants of the prison affords a very striking view of the practices predominant in *Shakespear's* age. Besides those whose follies are common to all times, we have four fighting men and a traveller. It is not unlikely that the originals of these pictures were then known.

ACT IV. SCENE xiii. (IV. v. 1.)

> DUKE. *These letters at fit time deliver me.*

Peter never delivers the letters, but tells his story without any credentials. The poet forgot the plot which he had formed.

ACT V. SCENE vii. (V. i. 448.)

> *'Till he did look on me.*

The *Duke* has justly observed that *Isabel* is *importuned against all sense* to solicit for *Angelo*, yet here *against all sense* she solicits for him. Her argument is extraordinary.

> *A due sincerity govern'd his deeds,*
> *'Till he did look on me ; since it is so,*
> *Let him not die.*

That *Angelo* had committed all the crimes charged against him, as far as he could commit them, is evident.

The only *intent* which *his act did not overtake*, was the defilement of *Isabel*. Of this *Angelo* was only intentionally guilty.

Angelo's crimes were such, as must sufficiently justify punishment, whether its end be to secure the innocent from wrong, or to deter guilt by example ; and I believe every reader feels some indignation when he finds him spared. From what extenuation of his crime can *Isabel*, who yet supposes her brother dead, form any plea in his favour. *Since he was good 'till he looked on me, let him not die*. I am afraid our Varlet Poet intended to inculcate, that women think ill of nothing that raises the credit of their beauty, and are ready, however virtuous, to pardon any act which they think incited by their own charms.

Act V. Scene viii. (v. i. 479 foll.)

It is somewhat strange, that *Isabel* is not made to express either gratitude, wonder or joy at the sight of her brother.

After the pardon of two murderers *Lucio* might be treated by the good *Duke* with less harshness ; but perhaps the Poet intended to show, what is too often seen, *that men easily forgive wrongs which are not committed against themselves*.

The novel of *Cynthio Giraldi*, from which *Shakespear* is supposed to have borrowed this fable, may be read in *Shakespear illustrated*, elegantly translated, with remarks which will assist the enquirer to discover how much absurdity *Shakespear* has admitted or avoided. I cannot but suspect that some other had new modelled the novel of *Cynthio*, or written a story which in some particulars resembled it, and that *Cinthio* was not the authour whom *Shakespear* immediately followed. The Emperour in *Cinthio* is named *Maximine*, the Duke, in *Shakespear*'s enumeration of the persons of the drama, is called *Vincentio*. This appears a very slight remark; but since the Duke has no name in the play, nor is ever mentioned but by his title, why should he be called *Vincentio* among the *Persons*, but because the name was copied from the story, and placed superfluously at the head of the list by the mere habit of transcription? It is therefore likely that there was then a story of *Vincentio* Duke of *Vienna*, different from that of *Maximine* Emperour of the *Romans*.

Of this play the light or comick part is very natural and pleasing, but the grave scenes, if a few passages be excepted, have more labour than elegance. The plot is rather intricate than artful. The time of the action is indefinite; some time, we know not how much, must have elapsed between the recess of the *Duke* and the imprisonment of *Claudio*; for he must have learned the story of *Mariana* in his disguise, or he delegated his power to a man already known to be corrupted. The unities of action and place are sufficiently preserved.

THE MERCHANT OF VENICE.

Act I. Scene ii. (i. ii. 48.)
There is the Count Palatine.

I am always inclined to believe, that *Shakespear* has more allusions to particular facts and persons than his readers commonly suppose. The Count here mentioned was, perhaps, *Albertus a Lasco*, a *Polish* Palatine, who visited *England* in our Authour's time, was eagerly caressed, and splendidly entertained, but running in debt, at last stole away, and endeavoured to repair his fortune by enchantment.

ACT II. SCENE viii. (II. vii. 78.)

> PORTIA. *A gentle riddance—draw the curtains ; go—*
> *Let all of his complexion chuse me so.*

The old quarto Edition of 1600 has no distribution
of acts, but proceeds from the beginning to the end in
an unbroken tenour. This play therefore having been
probably divided without authority by the publishers
of the first folio, lies open to a new regulation if any
more commodious division can be proposed. The
story is itself so wildly incredible, and the changes of
the scene so frequent and capricious, that the probability of action does not deserve much care ; yet it
may be proper to observe, that, by concluding the
second act here, time is given for *Bassanio's* passage
to *Belmont.*

ACT V. SCENE i. (V. i. 32–3.)

> LORENZO. *Who comes with her ?*
> MESSENGER. *None, but a holy hermit, and her maid.*

I do not perceive the use of this hermit, of whom
nothing is seen or heard afterwards. The Poet had
first planned his fable some other way, and inadvertently, when he changed his scheme, retained something of the original design.

Of *The* MERCHANT *of* VENICE the stile is even and
easy, with few peculiarities of diction, or anomalies of
construction. The comick part raises laughter, and
the serious fixes expectation. The probability of
either one or the other story cannot be maintained.
The union of two actions in one event is in this drama
eminently happy. *Dryden* was much pleased with his
own address in connecting the two plots of his
Spanish Friar, which yet, I believe, the critick will find
excelled by this play.

AS YOU LIKE IT.

Act II. Scene i. (ii. i. 12–14.)

> *Sweet are the uses of Adversity,*
> *Which, like the toad, ugly and venomous,*
> *Wears yet a precious jewel in his head.*

It was the current opinion in *Shakespeare*'s time, that in the head of an old toad was to be found a stone, or pearl, to which great virtues were ascribed. This stone has been often sought, but nothing has been found more than accidental or perhaps morbid indurations of the skull.

Act II. Scene viii. (ii. vii. 94–6.)

> *The thorny point*
> *Of sharp distress has ta'en from me the shew*
> *Of smooth civility.*

We might read *torn* with more elegance, but elegance alone will not justify alteration.

Act II. Scene x. (ii. vii. 167.)

> *Set down your venerable burthen.*

Is it not likely that *Shakespear* had in his mind this line of the *Metamorphoses?*

> ———— *Patremque*
> *Fert humerus*, venerabile onus *Cythereius heros.*

Act III. Scene ii. (iii. ii. 2.)

> *Thrice crowned Queen of Night.*

Alluding to the triple character of *Proserpine*, *Cynthia*, and *Diana*, given by some Mythologists to the same Goddess, and comprised in these memorial lines :

> *Terret, lustrat, agit, Proserpina, Luna, Diana,*
> *Ima, superna, feras, sceptro, fulgore, sagittis.*

Act III. **Scene** v. (III. ii. 136-7.)

> *Tongues I'll hang on every tree,*
> *That shall civil sayings show.*

Civil is here used in the same sense as when we say *civil* wisdom or *civil* life, in opposition to a solitary state, or to the state of nature. This desart shall not appear *unpeopled*, for every tree shall teach the maxims or incidents of social life.

Act III. **Scene** v. (III. ii. 150-2.)

> *Therefore heaven nature charg'd,*
> *That one body should be fill'd*
> *With all graces wide enlarged.*

From the picture of *Apelles*, or the accomplishments of *Pandora*.

> Πανδώρην, ὅτι πάντες ὀλύμπια δώματ' ἔχοντες
> Δῶρον ἐδώρησαν.———

So before,

> ——————————— *But thou*
> *So perfect, and so peerless art counted*
> *Of ev'ry creature's best.*—Tempest.

Perhaps from this passage *Swift* had his hint of *Biddy Floyd*.

Act III. **Scene** v. (III. ii. 156.)

> *Atalanta's better part.*

I know not well what could be the better part of *Atalanta* here ascribed to *Rosalind*. Of the *Atalanta* most celebrated, and who therefore must be intended here where she has no epithet of discrimination, the *better part* seems to have been her heels, and the worse part was so bad that *Rosalind* would not thank her lover for the comparison. There is a more obscure *Atalanta*, a Huntress and a Heroine, but of her nothing bad is recorded, and therefore I know not which was the better part. *Shakespeare* was no despicable Mythologist, yet he seems here to have mistaken some other character for that of *Atalanta*.

Act III. Scene vi. (III. ii. 187-8.)

I was never so be-rhymed since Pythagoras *time, that I was an* Irish *rat.*

Rosalind is a very learned Lady. She alludes to the *Pythagorean* doctrine which teaches that souls transmigrate from one animal to another, and relates that in his time she was an *Irish rat*, and by some metrical charm was rhymed to death. The power of killing rats with rhymes *Donne* mentions in his satires, and *Temple* in his treatises. Dr. *Gray* has produced a similar passage from *Randolph*

——— *My Poets*
Shall with a satire steeped in vinegar
Rhyme them to death, as they do rats in Ireland.

Act III. Scene x. (III. iv.)

There is much of nature in this petty perverseness of *Rosalind* ; she finds faults in her lover, in hope to be contradicted, and when *Celia* in sportive malice too readily seconds her accusations, she contradicts herself, rather than suffer her favourite to want a vindication.

Act IV. Scene i. (IV. i. 39-40.)

I will scarce think you have swam in a Gondola.

That is, *been at* Venice, the seat at that time of all licentiousness, where the young *English* gentlemen wasted their fortunes, debased their morals, and sometimes lost their religion.

The fashion of travelling which prevailed very much in our author's time, was considered by the wiser men as one of the principal causes of corrupt manners. It was therefore gravely censured by *Ascham* in his *School-master*, and by Bishop *Hall* in his *Quo Vadis*, and is here, and in other passages ridiculed by *Shakespeare*.

Of this play the fable is wild and pleasing. I know not how the ladies will approve the facility with which both *Rosalind* and *Celia* give away their hearts. To *Celia* much may be forgiven for the heroism of her friendship. The character of *Jaques* is natural and well preserved. The comick dialogue is very sprightly, with less mixture of low buffoonery than in some other plays ; and the graver part is elegant and harmonious. By hastening to the end of his work *Shakespeare* suppressed the dialogue between the usurper and the hermit, and lost an opportunity of exhibiting a moral lesson in which he might have found matter worthy of his highest powers.

LOVE'S LABOUR'S LOST.

The stile of the rhyming scenes in this play is often entangled and obscure.

ACT I. SCENE i. (I. i. 77.)
> *Light, seeking light, doth light of light beguile.*

The whole sense of this gingling declamation is only this, that *a man by too close study may read himself blind*, which might have been told with less obscurity in fewer words.

ACT I. SCENE i. (I. i. 148.)
> *Necessity will make us all forsworn.*

Biron amidst his extravagancies, speaks with great justness against the folly of vows. They are made without sufficient regard to the variations of life, and are therefore broken by some unforseen necessity. They proceed commonly from a presumptuous confidence, and a false estimate of human power.

Act I. Scene iii. (I. ii. 5.) *Dear imp.*

Imp was anciently a term of dignity. Lord *Cromwel* in his last letter to *Henry* VIII. prays for *the* imp *his son.* It is now used only in contempt or abhorrence; perhaps in our authour's time it was ambiguous, in which state it suits well with this dialogue.

Act II. Scene ii. (II. i. 221.)
      My lips are no common, though several they be.

Several is an inclosed field of a private proprietor, so *Maria* says, *her lips* are *private property.* Of a Lord that was newly married one observed that he grew fat; yes, said Sir *Walter Raleigh*, any beast will grow fat, if you take him from the *common* and graze him in the *several.*

Act IV. Scene ii. (IV. ii.) *Holophernes.*

I am not of the learned commentator's opinion, that the satire of *Shakespeare* is so seldom personal. It is of the nature of personal invectives to be soon unintelligible; and the authour that gratifies private malice, *animam in volnere ponit,* destroys the future efficacy of his own writings, and sacrifices the esteem of succeeding times to the laughter of a day. It is no wonder, therefore, that the sarcasms which, perhaps, in the authour's time *set the* playhouse *in a roar*, are now lost among general reflections. Yet whether the character of *Holofernes* was pointed at any particular man, I am, notwithstanding the plausibility of Dr. *Warburton*'s conjecture, inclined to doubt. Every man adheres as long as he can to his own pre-conceptions.

Before I read this note I considered the character of *Holofernes* as borrowed from the *Rhombus* of Sir *Philip Sidney*, who, in a kind of pastoral entertainment exhibited to Queen *Elizabeth*, has introduced a schoolmaster so called, speaking *a leash of languages at once*, and puzzling himself and his auditors with a jargon like that of *Holofernes* in the present play. *Sidney* himself might bring the character from *Italy*; for as *Peacham* observes, the Schoolmaster has long been one of the ridiculous personages in the farces of that country.

ACT V. SCENE i. (v. i. 2–6.)

NATHANIEL. *I praise God for you, Sir, your reasons at dinner have been sharp and sententious; pleasant without scurrility, witty without affectation, audacious without impudency, learned without opinion, and strange without heresy.*

I know not well what degree of respect *Shakespeare* intends to obtain for this vicar, but he has here put into his mouth a finished representation of colloquial excellence. It is very difficult to add any thing to this character of the schoolmaster's table-talk, and perhaps all the precepts of *Castiglione* will scarcely be found to comprehend a rule for conversation so justly delineated, so widely dilated, and so nicely limited.

It may be proper just to note, that *reason* here, and in many other places, signifies *discourse*, and that *audacious* is used in a good sense for *spirited, animated, confident*. *Opinion* is the same with *obstinacy* or *opiniatreté*.

ACT V. SCENE iii. (v. ii. 69–72.)

PRINCESS. *None are so surely caught, when they are catch'd,*
　　　　As wit turn'd fool: folly, in wisdom hatch'd,
　　　　Hath wisdom's warrant, and the help of school;
　　　　And wit's own grace to grace a learned fool.

These are observations worthy of a man who has surveyed human nature with the closest attention.

ACT V. SCENE v. (v. ii. 206.)
> *Vouchsafe, bright moon, and these thy stars, to shine.*

When Queen *Elizabeth* asked an ambassadour how he liked her Ladies, *It is hard*, said he, *to judge of stars in the presence of the sun.*

ACT V. SCENE viii. (v. ii. 374-9.)
> BIRON.   *Fair, gentle, sweet,*
> *Your wit makes wise things foolish ; when we greet*
> *With eyes best seeing heaven's fiery eye,*
> *By light we lose light ; your capacity*
> *Is of that nature, as to your huge store*
> *Wise things seem foolish, and rich things but poor.*

This is a very lofty and elegant compliment.

In this play, which all the editors have concurred to censure, and some have rejected as unworthy of our Poet, it must be confessed that there are many passages mean, childish, and vulgar ; and some which ought not to have been exhibited, as we are told they were, to a maiden queen.   But there are scattered, through the whole, many sparks of genius ; nor is there any play that has more evident marks of the hand of *Shakespeare.*

THE WINTER'S TALE.

ACT I. SCENE iii. (I. ii. 260-1.)
> *Whereof the execution did cry out*
> *Against the non-performance.*

This is one of the expressions by which *Shakespeare* too frequently clouds his meaning.   This sounding phrase means, I think, no more than *a thing necessary to be done.*

Act III. Scene ii. (III. ii. 55–8.)

> *I ne'er heard yet,*
> *That any of those bolder vices* wanted
> Less *impudence to gainsay what they did,*
> *Than to perform it first.*

It is apparent that according to the proper, at least according to the present, use of words, *less* should be *more*, or *wanted* should be *had*. But *Shakespeare* is very uncertain in his use of negatives. It may be necessary once to observe, that in our language two negatives did not originally affirm, but strengthen the negation. This mode of speech was in time changed, but as the change was made in opposition to long custom, it proceeded gradually, and uniformity was not obtained but through an intermediate confusion.

Act III. Scene iv. (III. ii. 152–73.)

This vehement retractation of *Leontes*, accompanied with the confession of more crimes than he was suspected of, is agreeable to our daily experience of the vicissitudes of violent tempers, and the eruptions of minds oppressed with guilt.

Act IV. Scene iv. (IV. iii. 21–2.)

> *How would he look, to see his work, so noble,*
> *Vilely bound up!*

It is impossible for any man to rid his mind of his profession. The authorship of *Shakespeare* has supplied him with a metaphor, which rather than he would lose it, he has put with no great propriety into the mouth of a country maid. Thinking of his own works his mind passed naturally to the Binder. I am glad that he has no hint at an Editor.

Act V. Scene v. (V. ii. 43–4.)

3 Gentleman.   *Did you see the meeting of the two Kings?*

It was, I suppose, only to spare his own labour that

the poet put this whole scene into narrative, for though part of the transaction was already known to the audience, and therefore could not properly be shewn again, yet the two kings might have met upon the stage, and after the examination of the old shepherd, the young Lady might have been recognized in sight of the spectators.

Of this play no edition is known published before the folio of 1623.

The story is taken from the novel of *Dorastus* and *Faunia*, which may be read in *Shakespeare illustrated.*

This play, as Dr. *Warburton* justly observes, is, with all its absurdities, very entertaining. The character of *Autolycus* is very naturally conceived, and strongly represented.

TWELFTH NIGHT.

Act I. Scene i. (I. i. 19, 21.)

> *O, when my eyes did see Olivia first,*
> *That instant I was turn'd into a hart.*

This image evidently alludes to the story of *Acteon*, by which *Shakespeare* seems to think men cautioned against too great familiarity with forbidden beauty. *Acteon*, who saw *Diana* naked, and was torn in pieces by his hounds, represents a man, who indulging his eyes, or his imagination, with the view of a woman that he cannot gain, has his heart torn with incessant longing. An interpretation far more elegant and natural than that of Sir *Francis Bacon*, who, in his *Wisdom of the Antients*, supposes this story to warn us against enquiring into the secrets of princes, by showing, that those who knew that which for reasons of state is to be concealed, will be detected and destroyed by their own servants.

Act I. Scene ii. (i. ii. 39.)

> *O, that I serv'd that lady &c.*

Viola seems to have formed a very deep design with very little premeditation : she is thrown by shipwreck on an unknown coast, hears that the prince is a batchelor, and resolves to supplant the lady whom he courts.

Act I. Scene ii. (i. ii. 53.) *I'll serve this Duke.*

Viola is an excellent schemer, never at a loss ; if she cannot serve the lady, she will serve the Duke.

Act II. Scene iv. (ii. iii. 86.) *Tilly valley.*

Tilly valley was an interjection of contempt, which Sir *Thomas More*'s lady is recorded to have had very often in her mouth.

Act II. Scene viii. (ii. v. 66–8.)

> Malvolio. *I frown the while, and, perchance, wind up my watch, or play with some rich jewel.*

In our authour's time watches were very uncommon. When *Guy Faux* was taken, it was urged as a circumstance of suspicion that a watch was found upon him.

Act III. Scene x. (iii. iv. 185–7.)

> Sir Toby. *Fare thee well, and God have mercy upon one of our souls : he may have mercy upon mine, but my hope is better.*

We may read, *He may have mercy upon* thine, *but my hope is better.* Yet the passage may well enough stand without alteration.

It were much to be wished, that *Shakespeare* in this and some other passages, had not ventured so near profaneness.

Act III. Scene xii. (iii. iv. 260–1.)

> *He is Knight, dubb'd with unhack'd rapier, and on carpet consideration.*

That is, he is no soldier by profession, not a Knight

Banneret, dubbed in the field of battle, but, *on carpet consideration*, at a festivity, or on some peaceable occasion, when knights receive their dignity kneeling not on the ground, as in war, but on a *carpet*. This is, I believe, the original of the contemptuous term a *carpet knight*, who was naturally held in scorn by the men of war.

ACT V. SCENE i. (v. i. 42.) *Bells of St. Bennet.*

When in this play he mentioned the *bed of* Ware, he recollected that the scene was in *Illyria*, and added *in England*; but his sense of the same impropriety could not restrain him from the bells of St. *Bennet*.

This play is in the graver part elegant and easy, and in some of the lighter scenes exquisitely humorous. *Ague-cheek* is drawn with great propriety, but his character is, in a great measure, that of natural fatuity, and is therefore not the proper prey of a satirist. The soliloquy of *Malvolio* is truly comick; he is betrayed to ridicule merely by his pride. The marriage of *Olivia*, and the succeeding perplexity, though well enough contrived to divert on the stage, wants credibility, and fails to produce the proper instruction required in the drama, as it exhibits no just picture of life.

THE MERRY WIVES OF WINDSOR.

ACT II. SCENE iv. (II. i. 147.)
    PAGE. *I will not believe such a* Cataian.

To be a foreigner was always in *England*, and I suppose every where else, a reason of dislike.

ACT II. SCENE viii. (II. ii. 94-5.) *A very frampold life.*

This word I have never seen elsewhere except in

Dr. *Hacket*'s life of Archbishop *Williams*, where a *frampul* man signifies a peevish troublesome fellow.

Аст III. Scene xii. (III. iv. 13–14.)
*Thy father's wealth
Was the first motive that I woo'd thee.*

Some light may be given to those who shall endeavour to calculate the encrease of *English* wealth, by observing, that *Latymer* in the time of *Edward* VI. mentions it as a proof of his father's prosperity, *That though but a yeoman, he gave his daughters five pounds each for her portion.* At the latter end of *Elizabeth*, seven hundred pounds were such a temptation to courtship, as made all other motives suspected. *Congreve* makes twelve thousand pounds more than a counterballance to the affectation of *Belinda*. No poet would now fly his favourite character at less than fifty thousand.

Аст III. Scene xvii. (III. v. 157–8.)   *I'll be horn-mad.*

There is no image which our authour appears so fond of as that of a cuckold's horns. Scarcely a light character is introduced that does not endeavour to produce merriment by some allusion to horned husbands. As he wrote his plays for the stage rather than the press, he perhaps reviewed them seldom, and did not observe this repetition, or finding the jest, however frequent, still successful, did not think correction necessary.

Аст IV. Scene v. (IV. ii. 208–9.)
I spy a great peard under her muffler.

As the second stratagem, by which *Falstaff* escapes, is much the grosser of the two, I wish it had been practised first. It is very unlikely that *Ford* having been so deceived before, and knowing that he had been deceived, would suffer him to escape in so slight a disguise.

ACT IV. SCENE vii. (IV. iii. 12–13.) *They must* COME *off*

To come off, signifies in our authour, sometimes *to be uttered with spirit and volubility*. In this place it seems to mean what is in our time expressed by *to come down*, to pay liberally and readily. These accidental and colloquial senses are the disgrace of language, and the plague of commentators.

ACT IV. SCENE x. (IV. v. 130.) *Good hearts.*

The great fault of this play is the frequency of expressions so profane, that no necessity of preserving character can justify them. There are laws of higher authority than those of criticism.

THE TAMING OF THE SHREW.

ACT. I. SCENE iv. (I. i. 166.)
> *Redime te captum quam queas minimo.*

Our author had this line from *Lilly*, which I mention, that it may not be brought as an argument of his learning.

ACT II. SCENE vi. (II. i. 331–2.)
> GREMIO. *Youngling ! thou canst not love so dear as I.*
> TRANIO. *Grey-beard ! thy love doth freeze.*
> GREMIO. *But thine doth fry.*

Old *Gremio*'s notions are confirmed by *Shadwell*.
> *The fire of love in youthful blood,*
> *Like what is kindled in brushwood,*
> *But for a moment burns——*
> *But when crept into aged veins,*
> *It slowly burns, and long remains,*

> *It glows, and with a sullen heat,*
> *Like fire in logs, it burns, and warms us long ;*
> *And though the flame be not so great*
> *Yet is the heat as strong.*

Act V. Scene iv. (v. ii. 54.)

PETRUCHIO.   *A good swift Simile.*

Swift, besides the original sense of *speedy in motion*, signified *witty, quick-witted.* So in *As you like it*, the Duke says of the clown, *He is very* swift *and sententious.* *Quick* is now used in almost the same sense, as *nimble* was in the age after that of our authour. *Heylin* says of *Hales*, that *he had known* Laud *for a* nimble *disputant.*

From this play the Tatler formed a story, Vol. 4. N°. 131.

It cannot but seem strange that *Shakespeare* should be so little known to the authour of the Tatler, that he should suffer this Story to be obtruded upon him, or so little known to the Publick, that he could hope to make it pass upon his readers as a novel narrative of a transaction in *Lincolnshire* ; yet it is apparent, that he was deceived, or intended to deceive, that he knew not himself whence the story was taken, or hoped that he might rob so obscure a writer without detection.

Of this play the two plots are so well united, that they can hardly be called two without injury to the art with which they are interwoven. The attention is entertained with all the variety of a double plot, yet is not distracted by unconnected incidents.

The part between *Catharine* and *Petruchio* is eminently spritely and diverting. At the marriage of *Bianca* the arrival of the real father, perhaps, produces more perplexity than pleasure. The whole play is very popular and diverting.

THE COMEDY OF ERRORS

Act III. Scene ii. (III. ii. 63-4.)

> Antipholis of Syracuse. *My food, my fortune, and my sweet hope's aim,*
> *My sole earth's heaven, and my heaven's claim.*

When he calls the girl his *only heaven on earth*, he utters the common cant of lovers. When he calls her *his heaven's claim*, I cannot understand him. Perhaps he means that which he asks of heaven.

MUCH ADO ABOUT NOTHING.

Act I. Scene i. (I. i. 67.)   *Four of his five wits.*

In our authour's time *wit* was the general term for intellectual powers. So *Davies* on the Soul,

> Wit, *seeking truth from cause to cause ascends,*
> *And never rests till it the first attain ;*
> Will, *seeking good, finds many middle ends,*
> *But never stays till it the last do gain.*

And in another part,

> *But if a phrenzy do possess the brain,*
> *It so disturbs and blots the form of things,*
> *As fantasy proves altogether vain,*
> *And to the* wit *no true relation brings.*
> *Then doth the* wit, *admitting all for true,*
> *Build fond conclusions on those idle grounds ;———*

The *wits* seem to have reckoned five, by analogy to the five senses, or the five inlets of ideas.

Act I. Scene vi. (I. iii. 14.)

> Don John. *I cannot hide what I am.*

This is one of our authour's natural touches. An envious and unsocial mind, too proud to give pleasure, and too sullen to receive it, always endeavours to hide its malignity from the world and from itself, under the plainness of simple honesty, or the dignity of haughty independence.

ACT II. SCENE v. (II. i. 332–4.)

Thus goes every one to the world but I, and I am sunburnt.

What is it, *to go to the world?* perhaps, to enter by marriage into a settled state : but why is the unmarried Lady *sunburnt?* I believe we should read, *thus goes every one to the* wood *but I, and I am sunburnt.* Thus does every one but I find a shelter, and I am left exposed to wind and *sun. The nearest way to the* wood, is a phrase for the readiest means to any end. It is said of a woman, who accepts a worse match than those which she had refused, that she has passed through the *wood*, and at last taken a crooked stick. But conjectural criticism has always something to abate its confidence. *Shakespeare*, in *All's well that ends well*, uses the phrase, *to go to the world*, for *marriage*. So that my emendation depends only on the opposition of *wood* to *sun-burnt*.

ACT III. SCENE iv. (III. iii. 43–4.)

DOGBERRY.   *Have a care that your Bills be not stolen.*

A *bill* is still carried by the watchmen at *Lichfield*. It was the old weapon of the *English* infantry, which, says *Temple*, *gave the most ghastly and deplorable wounds*. It may be called *securis falcata*.

ACT IV. SCENE ii. (IV. i. 251–2.)

LEONATO.   *Being that I flow in grief,*
The smallest twine may lead me.

This is one of our authour's observations upon life. Men over-powered with distress eagerly listen to the first offers of relief, close with every scheme, and believe every promise. He that has no longer any confidence in himself, is glad to repose his trust in any other that will undertake to guide him.

ALL'S WELL THAT ENDS WELL.

Act I. Scene i. (I. i. 49–52.)

Where an unclean mind carries virtuous qualities, there commendations go with pity, they are virtues and traitors too ; in her they are the better for their simpleness.

Estimable and useful qualities, joined with evil disposition, give that evil disposition power over others, who, by admiring the virtue, are betrayed to the malevolence. The *Tatler*, mentioning the sharpers of his time, observes, that some of them are men of such elegance and knowledge, that *a young man who falls into their way is* betrayed *as much by his judgment as his passions.*

Act I. Scene v. (I. ii. 36–8.)

7431

7438

> *So like a Courtier, no Contempt or Bitterness*
> *Were in his Pride or Sharpness ; or if they were,*
> *His Equal had awak'd them.*

He was so like a courtier, that there was in *his dignity of manner nothing contemptuous,* and *in his keenness of wit nothing bitter.* If *bitterness* or *contemptuousness* ever *appeared,* they had been *awakened* by some injury, not of a man below him, but of his *Equal.* This is the complete image of a well bred man, and somewhat like this *Voltaire* has exhibited his hero *Lewis* XIV.

Act I. Scene v. (I. ii. 41–5.)

> *Who were below him*
> *He us'd as creatures of another place,*
> *And bow'd his eminent top to their low ranks ;*
> *Making them proud of his humility,*
> *In their poor praise he humbled.*

Every man has seen the *mean* too often *proud of the humility* of the great, and perhaps the great may sometimes be *humbled in the praises* of the mean, of those who commend them without conviction or discernment : this, however is not so common ; the *mean* are found more frequently than the *great*.

ACT I. SCENE vi. (I. iii. s.d.)   *Steward and* Clown.

A *Clown* in *Shakespeare* is commonly taken for a *licensed jester*, or domestick *fool*. We are not to wonder that we find this character often in his plays, since fools were, at that time, maintained in all great families, to keep up merriment in the house. In the picture of Sir *Thomas Moore*'s family, by *Hans Holbein*, the only servant represented is *Patison* the *fool*. This is a proof of the familiarity to which they were admitted, not by the great only, but the wise.

In some plays, a servant, or rustic, of remarkable petulance and freedom of speech, is likewise called a *Clown*.

ACT I. SCENE vi. (I. iii. 98–101.)

Tho' honesty be no puritan, yet it will do no hurt ; it will wear the surplice of humility over the black gown of a big heart.

Here is an allusion, violently enough forced in, to satirise the obstinacy with which the *Puritans* refused the use of the ecclesiastical habits, which was, at that time, one principal cause of the breach of union, and, perhaps, to insinuate, that the modest purity of the surplice was sometimes a cover for pride.

ACT IV. SCENE ii. (IV. ii. 73–4.)

DIANA.   *Since Frenchmen are so braid,*
          Marry that will, I'll live and die a Maid.

Nothing is more common than for girls, on such occasions, to say in a pett what they do not think, or to think for a time what they do not finally resolve.

ACT IV. SCENE iii. (IV. iii. I.)   *First Lord.*

The later Editors have with great liberality bestowed lordship upon these interlocutors, who, in the original edition, are called, with more propriety, *capt.* E. and *capt.* G.   It is true that *captain* E. is in a former scene called *Lord E.* but the subordination in which they seem to act, and the timorous manner in which they converse, determines them to be only captains.   Yet as the later readers of *Shakespeare* have been used to find them lords, I have not thought it worth while to degrade them in the margin.

ACT IV. SCENE v. (IV. iii. 282.)
He will steal, Sir, an egg out of a cloister.

I know not that *cloister*, though it may etymologically signify *any thing shut* is used by our authour, otherwise than for a *monastery*, and therefore I cannot guess whence this hyberbole could take its original : perhaps it means only this : *He will steal any thing, however trifling, from any place, however holy.*

ACT V. SCENE ii. (V. ii. 58–9.)
Tho' you are a fool and a knave, you shall eat.

Parolles has many of the lineaments of *Falstaff*, and seems to be the character which *Shakespeare* delighted to draw, a fellow that had more wit than virtue. Though justice required that he should be detected and exposed, yet his *vices sit so fit in him* that he is not at last suffered to starve.

ACT V. SCENE iii. (V. iii. 20–2.)
KING.   *Call him hither ;*
          We're reconcil'd, and the first view shall kill
          All repetition.

The first interview shall put an end to all recollection

of the past.   Shakespeare is now hastening to the end
of the play, finds his matter sufficient to fill up his
remaining scenes, and therefore, as on other such
occasions, contracts his dialogue and precipitates his
action.   Decency required that *Bertram's* double
crime of cruelty and disobedience joined likewise with
some hypocrisy, should raise more resentment ; and
that though his mother might easily forgive him, his
king should more pertinaciously vindicate his own
authority and *Helen's* merit : of all this *Shakespeare*
could not be ignorant, but *Shakespeare* wanted to
conclude his play.

ACT V.   SCENE iv.   (v. iii. 93.)
    BERTRAM.   *In* Florence *was it from a casement thrown me.*

Bertram still continues to have too little virtue to
deserve *Helen.*   He did not know indeed that it was
Helen's ring, but he knew that he had it not from
a window.

ACT V.   SCENE iv.   (v. iii. 101-2.)
        Plutus himself,
        That knows the tinct and multiplying medicine.

In the reign of *Henry* the fourth a law was made to
forbid *all men thenceforth to* multiply *gold, or use any
craft of* multiplication.   Of which law Mr. *Boyle,* when
he was warm with the hope of transmutation, procured
a repeal.

ACT V.   SCENE vi.   (v. iii. 271-309.)

This dialogue [between the King and Diana] is too
long, since the audience already knew the whole
transaction ; nor is there any reason for puzzling the
king and playing with his passions ; but it was much
easier than to make a pathetical interview between
Helen and her husband, her mother, and the king.

This play has many delightful scenes, though not sufficiently probable, and some happy characters, though not new, nor produced by any deep knowledge of human nature. *Parolles* is a boaster and a coward, such as has always been the sport of the stage, but perhaps never raised more laughter or contempt than in the hands of *Shakespeare*.

I cannot reconcile my heart to *Bertram*; a man noble without generosity, and young without truth; who marries *Helen* as a coward, and leaves her as a profligate: when she is dead by his unkindness, sneaks home to a second marriage, is accused by a woman whom he has wronged, defends himself by falshood, and is dismissed to happiness.

The story of *Bertram* and *Diana* had been told before of *Mariana* and *Angelo*, and, to confess the truth, scarcely merited to be heard a second time.

The story is copied from a novel of *Boccace*, which may be read in *Shakespear Illustrated*, with remarks not more favourable to *Bertram* than my own.

KING JOHN.

ACT I. SCENE i. (I. i. 24–6.)

> KING JOHN.   *Be thou as lightning in the eyes of* France,
> *For ere thou canst report I will be there,*
> *The thunder of my cannon shall be heard.*

The simile does not suit well: the lightning indeed appears before the thunder is heard, but the lightning is destructive, and the thunder innocent.

ACT I. SCENE i. (I. i. 27–8.)

> *Be thou the trumpet of our wrath,*
> *And sullen presage of your own decay.*

By the epithet *sullen*, which cannot be applied to a trumpet, it is plain, that our authour's imagination had now suggested a new idea. It is as if he had said, be a *trumpet* to alarm with our invasion, be a *bird* of *ill omen* to croak out the prognostick of your own ruin.

Act I. Scene iv. (I. i. 225.) *Colbrand the giant.*

Colbrand was a *Danish* giant, whom *Guy* of *Warwick* discomfited in the presence of king *Athelstan.* The combat is very pompously described by *Drayton* in his *Polyolbion.*

Act II. Scene iv. (II. i. 300 foll.)
FRENCH HERALD. *Ye men of* Angiers, &c.

This speech is very poetical and smooth, and except the conceit of the *widow's husband* embracing *the earth,* is just and beautiful.

Act II. Scene v. (II. i. 477–9.)
> *Lest zeal now melted by the windy breath*
> *Of soft petitions, pity and remorse,*
> *Cool and congeal again to what it was.*

We have here a very unusual, and, I think, not very just image of *zeal,* which in its highest degree is represented by others as a flame, but by *Shakespeare* as a frost. To *repress* zeal, in the language of others, is to *cool,* in *Shakespeare's* to *melt* it; when it exerts its utmost power it is commonly said to *flame,* but by *Shakespeare* to be *congealed.*

Act III. Scene i. (III. i. 70–1.)
CONSTANCE. *To me, and to the State of my great Grief,*
>   *Let Kings assemble.*

In *Much ado about nothing,* the father of *Hero,* depressed by her disgrace, declares himself so subdued by grief that *a thread may lead him.* How is it that grief in *Leonato* and lady *Constance,* produces effects directly opposite, and yet both agreeable to nature.

Sorrow softens the mind while it is yet warmed by hope, but hardens it when it is congealed by despair. Distress, while there remains any prospect of relief, is weak and flexible, but when no succour remains, is fearless and stubborn ; angry alike at those that injure, and at those that do not help ; careless to please where nothing can be gained, and fearless to offend when there is nothing further to be dreaded. Such was this writer's knowledge of the passions.

ACT III. SCENE ii. (III. i. 75-134.)

What was the ground of this quarrel of the Bastard to *Austria* is no where specify'd in the present play ; nor is there in this place, or the scene where it is first hinted at (namely the second of Act 2.) the least mention of any reason for it. But the story is, that *Austria*, who kill'd King *Richard Cœur-de-lion*, wore as the spoil of that Prince, a lion's hide which had belong'd to him. This circumstance renders the anger of the Bastard very natural, and ought not to have been omitted. In the first sketch of this play (which *Shakespeare* is said to have had a hand in, jointly with *William Rowley*) we accordingly find this insisted upon, and I have ventured to place a few of those verses here.—POPE.

To the insertion of these lines I have nothing to object. There are many other passages in the old play, of great value. The omission of this incident, in the second draught, was natural. *Shakespeare*, having familiarised the story to his own imagination, forgot that it was obscure to his audience ; or, what is equally probable, the story was then so popular that a hint was sufficient at that time to bring it to mind, and these plays were written with very little care for the approbation of posterity.

ACT III. SCENE iii. (III. i. 149-51.)

KING JOHN. *Thou canst not, Cardinal, devise a name*
So slight, unworthy, and ridiculous,
To charge me to an answer, as the Pope.

This must have been at the time when it was written, in our struggles with popery, a very captivating scene.

So many passages remain in which *Shakespeare* evidently takes his advantage of the facts then recent, and of the passions then in motion, that I cannot but suspect that time has obscured much of his art, and that many allusions yet remain undiscovered which perhaps may be gradually retrieved by succeeding commentators.

ACT III. SCENE iii. (III. i. 204–6.)

LEWIS.   *Bethink you, father ; for the difference*
           Is purchase of a heavy curse from Rome.
           Or the light loss of England *for a friend.*

It is a political maxim, that *kingdoms are never married.* *Lewis* upon the wedding is for making war upon his new relations.

ACT III. SCENE iii. (III. i. 280 foll.)

PANDULPH.   *But thou hast sworn against religion, &c.*

In this long speech, the Legate is made to shew his skill in casuistry ; and the strange heap of quibble and nonsense of which it consists, was intended to ridicule that of the schools.—WAR-BURTON.

I am not able to discover here any thing inconsequent or ridiculously subtle. The propositions, that the *voice of the church is the voice of heaven,* and that *the Pope utters the voice of the church,* neither of which *Pandulph*'s auditors would deny, being once granted, the argument here used is irresistible ; nor is it easy, notwithstanding the gingle, to enforce it with greater brevity or propriety.

In swearing by religion against religion, to which thou hast already sworn, thou makest an oath the security for thy faith against an oath already taken. I will give, *says he,* a rule for conscience in these cases. Thou mayst be in doubt about the matter of an oath ; *when thou swearest thou mayst* not *be always* sure *to swear rightly,* but let this be thy settled principle, *swear only not to be forsworn*; let not thy latter oaths be at variance with thy former.

Truth, through this whole speech, means *rectitude* of conduct.

ACT III. SCENE iv. (III. ii. 1–3.)

> *Now, by my life, this day grows wond'rous hot;*
> *Some airy devil hovers in the sky,*
> *And pours down mischief.*

We must read, *Some* fiery *devil*, if we will have the *cause* equal to the *effect.*—WARBURTON.

There is no end of such alterations; every page of a vehement and negligent writer will afford opportunities for changes of terms, if mere propriety will justify them. Not that of this change the propriety is out of controversy. Dr. *Warburton* will have the devil *fiery*, because he makes the day *hot*; the authour makes him *airy*, because *he hovers in the sky*, and the *heat* and *mischief* are natural consequences of his malignity.

ACT III. SCENE vi. (III. iv. 61.)

> KING PHILIP. *Bind up those tresses.*

It was necessary that *Constance* should be interrupted, because a passion so violent cannot be born long. I wish the following speeches had been equally happy; but they only serve to shew, how difficult it is to maintain the pathetick long.

ACT III. SCENE vi. (III. iv. 99–100.)

> CONSTANCE. *Had you such a loss as I,*
> *I could give better comfort.*

This is a sentiment which great sorrow always dictates. Whoever cannot help himself casts his eyes on others for assistance, and often mistakes their inability for coldness.

ACT III. SCENE vii. (III. iv. 107.)

LEWIS. *There's nothing in this world can make me joy.*

The young Prince feels his defeat with more sensibility than his father. Shame operates most strongly in the earlier years, and when can disgrace be less welcome than when a man is going to his bride?

ACT III. SCENE vii. (III. iv. 176-7.)

> *As a little snow, tumbled about,*
> *Anon becomes a mountain.*

Bacon, in his history of *Henry* VII. speaking of *Perkin*'s march, observes, that *their* snow-ball *did not gather as it rolled.*

ACT IV. SCENE i. (IV. i. 101-2.)

ARTHUR. *Or*, Hubert, *if you will, cut out my tongue,*
So I may keep mine eyes.

This is according to nature. We imagine no evil so great as that which is near us.

ACT IV. SCENE iv. (IV. ii. 197-8.)

> *Slippers, which his nimble haste*
> *Had falsely thrust upon contrary feet.*

I know not how the commentators understand this important passage, which, in Dr. *Warburton*'s edition, is marked as eminently beautiful, and, in the whole, not without justice. But *Shakespeare* seems to have confounded a man's shoes with his gloves. He that is frighted or hurried may put his hand into the wrong glove, but either shoe will equally admit either foot. The authour seems to be disturbed by the disorder which he describes.

ACT IV. SCENE iv. (IV. ii. 231-5.)

KING JOHN. *Hadst thou but shook thy head, or made a pause, ...*
Deep shame had struck me dumb.

There are many touches of nature in this conference

of *John* with *Hubert*. A man engaged in wickedness would keep the profit to himself, and transfer the guilt to his accomplice. These reproaches vented against *Hubert* are not the words of art or policy, but the eruptions of a mind swelling with consciousness of a crime, and desirous of discharging its misery on another.

This account of the timidity of guilt is drawn *ab ipsis recessibus mentis*, from an intimate knowledge of mankind, particularly that line in which he says, that *to have bid him tell his tale* in *express words*, would have *struck him dumb*; nothing is more certain, than that bad men use all the arts of fallacy upon themselves, palliate their actions to their own minds by gentle terms, and hide themselves from their own detection in ambiguities and subterfuges.

The tragedy of *King John*, though not written with the utmost power of *Shakespeare*, is varied with a very pleasing interchange of incidents and characters. The Lady's grief is very affecting, and the character of the *Bastard* contains that mixture of greatness and levity which this authour delighted to exhibit.

There is extant another play of *King John*, published with *Shakespeare*'s name, so different from this, and I think from all his other works, that there is reason to think his name was prefixed only to recommend it to sale. No man writes upon the same subject twice, without concurring in many places with himself.

RICHARD II.

ACT I. SCENE v. (I. iii. 227-8.)

> GAUNT. *Shorten my days thou canst with sullen sorrow,*
> *And pluck nights from me, but not lend a morrow.*

It is matter of very melancholy consideration, that all human advantages confer more power of doing evil than good.

ACT II. SCENE i. (II. i. 21.)

> *Report of fashions in proud* Italy.

Our authour, who gives to all nations the customs of *England*, and to all ages the manners of his own ; has charged the times of *Richard* with a folly not perhaps known then, but very frequent in *Shakespeare*'s time, and much lamented by the wisest and best of our ancestors.

ACT III. SCENE ii. (III. ii. 56-7.)

> K. RICHARD. *The breath of worldly men cannot depose*
> *The Deputy elected by the Lord.*

Here is the doctrine of indefeasible right expressed in the strongest terms, but our poet did not learn it in the reign of King *James*, to which it is now the practice of all writers, whose opinions are regulated by fashion or interest, to impute the original of every tenet which they have been taught to think false or foolish.

ACT III. SCENE iv. (III. ii. 93.)

> K. RICHARD. *Mine ear is open, and my heart prepar'd.*

It seems to be the design of the poet to raise *Richard* to esteem in his fall, and consequently to interest the reader in his favour. He gives him only passive fortitude, the virtue of a confessor rather than of a king. In his prosperity we saw him imperious and oppressive, but in his distress he is wise, patient, and pious.

ACT III. SCENE iv. (III. ii. 153-4.)
> *That small model of the barren earth,*
> *Which serves as paste and cover to our bones.*

A metaphor, not of the most sublime kind, taken from a *pie*.

ACT III. SCENE iv. (III. ii. 207-8.)
> K. RICHARD. *By heav'n, I'll hate him everlastingly,*
> *That bids me be of comfort any more.*

This sentiment is drawn from nature. Nothing is more offensive to a mind convinced that his distress is without a remedy, and preparing to submit quietly to irresistible calamity, than these petty and conjectured comforts which unskilful officiousness thinks it virtue to administer.

ACT III. SCENE vi. (III. iii. 155-7.)
> K. RICHARD. *Or I'll be buried in the King's high way,*
> *Some way of common Trade, where Subjects' feet*
> *May hourly trample on their Sovereign's head.*

Shakespeare is very apt to deviate from the *pathetick* to the *ridiculous*. Had the speech of *Richard* ended at this line it had exhibited the natural language of submissive misery, conforming its intention to the present fortune, and calmly ending its purposes in death.

ACT IV. SCENE i. (IV. i. 39-40.)
> FITZWATER. *I will turn thy falsehood to thy heart,*
> *Where it was forged, with my rapier's point.*

Shakespeare deserts the manners of the age in which his drama is placed very often, without necessity or advantage. The edge of a sword had served his purpose as well as the *point of a rapier*, and he had then escaped the impropriety of giving the *English* nobles a weapon which was not seen in *England* till two centuries afterwards.

ACT IV. SCENE ii. (IV. i. 125–8.)

> CARLISLE.   *And shall the Figure of God's Majesty,*
> *His Captain, Steward, Deputy elect, . . .*
> *Be judg'd by subject and inferior breath?*

Here is another proof that our authour did not learn in King *James*'s court his elevated notions of the right of kings. I know not any flatterer of the *Stuarts* who has expressed this doctrine in much stronger terms. It must be observed that the Poet intends from the beginning to the end to exhibit this bishop as brave, pious, and venerable.

ACT IV. SCENE iv. (IV. i. 322–3.)

> CARLISLE.   *The children yet unborn,*
> *Shall feel this day as sharp to them as thorn.*

This pathetick denunciation shews that *Shakespeare* intended to impress his auditors with dislike of the deposal of *Richard*.

ACT V. SCENE i. (V. i. 46.)

> *For why? the senseless brands will sympathize.*

The poet should have ended this speech with the foregoing line, and have spared his childish prattle about the fire.

This play is extracted from the Chronicle of *Hollingshead*, in which many passages may be found which *Shakespeare* has, with very little alteration, transplanted into his scenes ; particularly a speech of the bishop of *Carlisle* in defence of King *Richard*'s unalienable right, and immunity from human jurisdiction.

Johnson, who, in his *Cataline* and *Sejanus*, has inserted many speeches from the *Roman* historians, was, perhaps, induced to that practice by the example of *Shakespeare*, who had condescended sometimes to copy more ignoble writers. But *Shakespeare* had more of his own than *Johnson*, and, if he sometimes was willing to spare his labour, shewed by what he performed at other times, that his extracts were made by choice or idleness rather than necessity.

This play is one of those which *Shakespeare* has apparently revised; but as success in works of invention is not always proportionate to labour, it is not finished at last with the happy force of some other of his tragedies, nor can be said much to affect the passions, or enlarge the understanding.

THE FIRST PART OF KING HENRY IV.

Shakespeare has apparently designed a regular connection of these dramatick histories from *Richard the second to Henry the fifth*. King *Henry*, at the end of *Richard* the second, declares his purpose to visit the Holy Land, which he resumes in this speech. The complaint made by king *Henry* in the last act of *Richard* the second, of the wildness of his son, prepares the reader for the frolicks which are here to be recounted, and the characters which are now to be exhibited.

Act I. Scene i. (1. i. 19.)
As far as to the sepulchre of Christ.

The lawfulness and justice of the *holy wars* have been much disputed; but perhaps there is a principle on which the question may be easily determined. If it be part of the religion of the Mahometans, to extirpate by the sword all other religions, it is, by the law of self defence, lawful for men of every other religion, and for Christians among others, to make war upon Mahometans, simply as Mahometans, as men obliged by their own principles to make war upon Christians, and only lying in wait till opportunity shall promise them success.

ACT I. SCENE iii. (I. ii. 217–18.)

PRINCE HENRY. *I know you all, and will a while uphold*
The unyok'd humour of your idleness.

This speech is very artfully introduced to keep the Prince from appearing vile in the opinion of the audience ; it prepares them for his future reformation, and, what is yet more valuable, exhibits a natural picture of a great mind offering excuses to itself, and palliating those follies which it can neither justify nor forsake.

ACT I. SCENE iv. (I. iii. 201–2.)

HOTSPUR. *By heav'n, methinks, it were an easy leap,*
To pluck bright honour from the pale-fac'd Moon.

Tho' the expression be sublime and daring, yet the thought is the natural movement of an heroic mind. *Euripides* at least thought so, when he put the very same sentiment, in the same words, into the mouth of *Eteocles*—*I will not, madam, disguise my thoughts ; I could scale heaven, I could descend to the very entrails of the earth, if so be that by that price I could obtain a kingdom.*— WARBURTON.

Though I am very far from condemning this speech with *Gildon* and *Theobald* as *absolute madness*, yet I cannot find in it that profundity of reflection and beauty of allegory which the learned commentator has endeavoured to display. This sally of *Hotspur* may be, I think, soberly and rationally vindicated as the violent eruption of a mind inflated with ambition and fired with resentment ; as the boastful clamour

of a man able to do much, and eager to do more ; as
the hasty motion of turbulent desire ; as the dark
expression of indetermined thoughts. The passage
from *Euripides* is surely not allegorical, yet it is produced, and properly, as parallel.

ACT I. SCENE iv. (I. iii. 287-8.)
> WORCESTER.   *The King will always think him in our debt,*
> *And think we deem ourselves unsatisfy'd.*

This is a natural description of the state of mind
between those that have conferred, and those that
have received, obligations too great to be satisfied.

That this would be the event of *Northumberland*'s
disloyalty was predicted by King *Richard* in the
former play.

ACT II. SCENE ii. (II. i. 95-6.)
> *We have the receipt of Fern-seed, we walk invisible.*

Fern is one of those plants which have their seed
on the back of the leaf so small as to escape the sight.
Those who perceived that *fern* was propagated by
semination and yet could never see the seed, were
much at a loss for a solution of the difficulty ; and as
wonder always endeavours to augment itself, they
ascribed to *Fern-seed* many strange properties ; some
of which the rustick virgins have not yet forgotten or
exploded.

ACT II. SCENE viii. (II. iv. 41-127.)   *Enter* Francis *the drawer.*

This scene, helped by the distraction of the drawer,
and grimaces of the prince, may entertain upon the
stage, but afford not much delight to the reader. The
authour has judiciously made it short.

ACT II. SCENE xi. (II. iv. 384-5.)
> PRINCE HENRY.   *He that rides at high speed, and with a pistol*
> *kills a sparrow flying.*

Shakespeare never has any care to preserve the

manners of the time. *Pistols* were not known in the
age of *Henry*. Pistols were, I believe, about our
authour's time, eminently used by the *Scots*. Sir
Henry Wotton somewhere makes mention of a *Scotish
pistol*.

Act II. Scene xi. (II. iv. 399–400.)

FALSTAFF. *You may buy land now as cheap as stinking
mackerel.*

In former times the prosperity of the nation was
known by the value of land as now by the price of
stocks. Before *Henry* the seventh made it safe to
serve the king regnant, it was the practice at every
revolution for the conqueror to confiscate the estates
of those that opposed, and perhaps of those who did
not assist him. Those, therefore, that foresaw a change
of government, and thought their estates in danger,
were desirous to sell them in haste for something that
might be carried away.

Act II. Scene xi. (II. iv. 446–7.)

FALSTAFF. *Though the camomile, the more it is trodden on, the
faster it grows.*

This whole speech is supremely comick. The simile
of camomile used to illustrate a contrary effect, brings
to my remembrance an observation of a later writer
of some merit, whom the desire of being witty has
betrayed into a like thought. Meaning to enforce
with great vehemence the mad temerity of young
soldiers, he remarks, that *though* Bedlam *be in the road
to* Hogsden, *it is out of the way to promotion.*

Act II. Scene xi. (II. iv. 557.)

PRINCE HENRY. *Go, hide thee behind the arras.*

The bulk of *Falstaff* made him not the fittest to be
concealed behind the hangings, but every poet sacri-

fices something to the scenery; if *Falstaff* had not been hidden he could not have been found asleep, nor had his pockets searched.

Aᴄᴛ III. Sᴄᴇɴᴇ i. (ɪɪɪ. i. 27-8.)

> Hᴏᴛsᴘᴜʀ. *Diseased Nature oftentimes breaks forth*
> *In strange eruptions.*

The poet has here taken, from the perverseness and contrariousness of *Hotspur*'s temper, an opportunity of raising his character, by a very rational and philosophical confutation of superstitious errour.

Aᴄᴛ III. Sᴄᴇɴᴇ i. (ɪɪɪ. i. 97-8.)

> Hᴏᴛsᴘᴜʀ. *Methinks, my moiety, north from Burton here,*
> *In quantity equals not one of yours.*

Hotspur is here just such a divider as the *Irishman* who made *three halves;* Therefore, for the honour of *Shakespeare*, I will suppose, with the *Oxford Editor*, that he wrote *portion.*—Wᴀʀ-ʙᴜʀᴛᴏɴ.

I will not suppose it.

Aᴄᴛ III. Sᴄᴇɴᴇ iv. (ɪɪɪ. ii. 66-7.)

> *To laugh at gybing boys, and stand the push*
> *Of every beardless, vain comparative.*

Of every boy whose vanity incited him to try his wit against the King's.

When *Lewis* XIV. was asked, why, with so much wit, he never attempted raillery, he answered, that he who practised raillery ought to bear it in his turn, and that to stand the butt of raillery was not suitable to the dignity of a King. *Scudery*'s Conversation.

Aᴄᴛ III. Sᴄᴇɴᴇ v. (ɪɪɪ. iii. 30.)

> Fᴀʟsᴛᴀꜰꜰ. *Thou art the Knight of the burning lamp.*

This is a natural picture. Every man who feels in himself the pain of deformity, however, like this merry knight, he may affect to make sport with it among those whom it is his interest to please, is ready to revenge any hint of contempt upon one whom he can use with freedom.

Act IV. Scene ii. (iv. i. 97–9.)

> *All furnisht, all in arms,*
> *All plum'd like Estridges, that with the wind*
> *Baited like Eagles.*

A more lively representation of young men ardent for enterprize perhaps no writer has ever given.

Act IV. Scene iii. (iv. ii. 21–2.)

> *Worse than a struck-fowl, or a hurt wild duck.*

The repetition of the same image disposed Sir *Tho. Hanmer*, and after him Dr. *Warburton*, to read, in opposition to all the copies, a struck *Deer*, which is indeed a proper expression, but not likely to have been corrupted. *Shakespeare*, perhaps, wrote a struck *sorel*, which, being negligently read by a man not skilled in hunter's language, was easily changed to struck *fowl*. *Sorel* is used in *Love's labour lost* for a young *deer*, and the terms of the chase were, in our authour's time, familiar to the ears of every gentleman.

Act IV. Scene iii. (iv. ii. 30–1.)

> *Younger sons to younger brothers.*

Raleigh, in his discourse on *war*, uses this very expression for men of desperate fortune and wild adventure. Which borrowed it from the other I know not, but I think the play was printed before the discourse.

THE SECOND PART OF KING HENRY IV.

INDUCTION.   *Enter* RUMOUR.

This speech of *Rumour* is not inelegant or unpoetical, but is wholly useless, since we are told nothing which the first scene does not clearly and naturally discover. The only end of such prologues is to inform the audience of some facts previous to the action, of which they can have no knowledge from the persons of the drama.

ACT I. SCENE iii. (I. i. 159–60.)

> *The rude scene may end,*
> *And darkness be the burier of the dead.*

The conclusion of this noble speech is extremely striking. There is no need to suppose it exactly philosophical, *darkness* in poetry may be absence of eyes as well as privation of light. Yet we may remark, that by an ancient opinion it has been held, that if the human race, for whom the world was made, were extirpated, the whole system of sublunary nature would cease.

ACT I. SCENE v. (I. ii. 166–8.)

FALSTAFF. *The young Prince hath mis-led me. I am the fellow with the great belly, and he my dog.*

I do not understand this joke. Dogs lead the blind, but why does a dog lead the fat?

ACT I. SCENE v. (I. ii. 208–10.)

CHIEF JUSTICE. *Is not your voice broken? your wind short? your chin double? your wit single?*

We call a man *single-witted* who attains but one species of knowledge. This sense I know not how to apply to *Falstaff*, and rather think that the *Chief Justice* hints at a calamity always incident to a gray-haired wit, whose misfortune is, that his merriment is unfashionable. His allusions are to forgotten facts; his illustrations are drawn from notions obscured by time; his *wit* is therefore *single*, such as none has any part in but himself.

ACT II. SCENE v. (II. ii. 98–9.)
> *Althea dream'd she was deliver'd of a firebrand.*

Shakespeare is here mistaken in his Mythology, and has confounded *Althea*'s firebrand with *Hecuba*'s. The firebrand of *Althea* was real; but *Hecuba*, when she was big with *Paris*, dreamed that she was delivered of a firebrand that consumed the kingdom.

ACT II. SCENE v. (II. ii. 189–91.)
> POINS. *Put on two leather jerkins and aprons, and wait upon him at his table, as drawers.*

This was a plot very unlikely to succeed where the *Prince* and the drawers were all known, but it produces merriment, which our authour found more useful than probability.

ACT III. SCENE v. (III. ii. 263–4.)
> BARDOLPH. *Sir, a word with you;—I have three pound to free* Mouldy *and* Bull-calf.

Here seems to be a wrong computation. He had forty shillings for each. Perhaps he meant to conceal part of the profit.

ACT IV. SCENE i. (IV. i. 24.)
> MOWBRAY. *Let us* sway *on, and face them in the field.*

I know not that I have ever seen *sway* in this sense, but I believe it is the true word, and was intended to express the uniform and forcible motion of a compact body. There is a sense of the noun in *Milton* kindred to this, where speaking of a weighty sword, he says, *It descends with huge two-handed* sway.

Act IV. Scene v. (iv. ii. 123)
    Lancaster. *Guard these traitors to the block of death.*

It cannot but raise some indignation to find this horrible violation of faith passed over thus slightly by the poet, without any note of censure or detestation.

Act IV. Scene vii. (iv. iii. 93-5.)
    Falstaff. *This same sober-blooded boy doth not love me, nor a man cannot make him laugh.*

Falstaff speaks here like a veteran in life. The young prince did not love him, and he despaired to gain his affection, for he could not make him laugh. Men only become friends by community of pleasures. He who cannot be softened into gayety cannot easily be melted into kindness.

Act IV. Scene xi. (iv. v. 127.)
    England *shall double gild his treble Guilt.*
    Evidently the nonsense of some foolish Player.—Warburton

I know not why this commentator should speak with so much confidence what he cannot know, or determine so positively what so capricious a writer as our poet might either deliberately or wantonly produce. This line is indeed such as disgraces a few that precede and follow it, but it suits well enough with the *daggers hid in thought, and whetted on the flinty hearts*; and the answer which the prince makes, and which is applauded for wisdom, is not of a strain much higher than this ejected line.

Act IV. Scene xi. (iv. v. 209.)
    To lead out many to the Holy Land.

This journey to the Holy Land, of which the king

very frequently revives the mention, had two motives, religion and policy. He durst not wear the ill-gotten crown without expiation, but in the act of expiation he contrives to make his wickedness successful.

ACT IV. SCENE xi. (IV. v. 217–18.)

KING HENRY.   *How I came by the Crown, O God, forgive!*
    And grant it may with thee in true peace live.

This is a true picture of a mind divided between heaven and earth. He prays for the prosperity of guilt while he deprecates its punishment.

ACT V. SCENE i. (v. i. 89.)   *Four terms or two actions.*

There is something humorous in making a spend-thrift compute time by the operation of an action for debt.

ACT V. SCENE i. (v. i. 90–3.)

O, it is much that a lie with a slight oath, and a jest with a sad brow, will do with a fellow that never had the ache in his shoulders.

That is, a *young fellow*, one whose disposition to merriment, time and pain have not yet impaired.

ACT V. SCENE iv. (v. iii. 60.)   *The cavaleroes about* London.

This was the term by which an airy splendid irregular fellow was distinguished. The soldiers of King *Charles* were called *Cavaliers* from the gayety which they affected in opposition to the sour faction of the parliament.

ACT V. SCENE iv. (v. iii. 80–1.)

SILENCE.   *An old man can do somewhat.*

It may be observed that *Shakespeare*, in the *Merry Wives of* Windsor, which he wrote after this play, for the greater commodiousness of his plot, changed the age of *Silence*. He is here a man advanced in years, with a son at the university : he there goes a courting to a young girl. *Shallow* is an old man in both plays.

ACT V. SCENE viii. (v. v. 68.)
KING. *I banish thee, on pain of death.*

Mr. *Rowe* observes, that many readers lament to see *Falstaff* so hardly used by his old friend. But if it be considered that the fat knight has never uttered one sentiment of generosity, and with all his power of exciting mirth, has nothing in him that can be esteemed, no great pain will be suffered from the reflection that he is compelled to live honestly, and maintained by the king, with a promise of advancement when he shall deserve it.

I think the poet more blameable for *Poins*, who is always represented as joining some virtues with his vices, and is therefore treated by the prince with apparent distinction, yet he does nothing in the time of action, and though after the bustle is over he is again a favourite, at last vanishes without notice. *Shakespeare* certainly lost him by heedlessness, in the multiplicity of his characters, the variety of his action, and his eagerness to end the play.

ACT V. SCENE ix. (v. v. 97.)
CHIEF JUSTICE. *Go, carry Sir* John Falstaff *to the* Fleet.

I do not see why *Falstaff* is carried to the Fleet. We have never lost sight of him since his dismission from the king ; he has committed no new fault, and therefore incurred no punishment ; but the different agitations of fear, anger, and surprise in him and his company, made a good scene to the eye ; and our authour, who wanted them no longer on the stage, was glad to find this method of sweeping them away.

I fancy every reader, when he ends this play, cries

out with *Desdemona, O most lame and impotent conclusion!* As this play was not, to our knowledge, divided
into acts by the authour, I could be content to conclude
it with the death of *Henry* the fourth.

In that Jerusalem shall Harry *dye.* These scenes
which now make the fifth act of *Henry* the fourth,
might then be the first of *Henry* the fifth; but the
truth is, that they do unite very commodiously to
either play. When these plays were represented,
I believe they ended as they are now ended in the
books; but *Shakespeare* seems to have designed that
the whole series of action from the beginning of *Richard*
the second, to the end of *Henry* the fifth, should be
considered by the reader as one work, upon one plan,
only broken into parts by the necessity of exhibition.

None of *Shakespeare's* plays are more read than the
first and second parts of *Henry* the fourth. Perhaps
no authour has ever in two plays afforded so much
delight. The great events are interesting, for the
fate of kingdoms depends upon them; the slighter
occurrences are diverting, and, except one or two,
sufficiently probable; the incidents are multiplied
with wonderful fertility of invention, and the characters diversified with the utmost nicety of discernment,
and the profoundest skill in the nature of man.

The prince, who is the hero both of the comick and
tragick part, is a young man of great abilities and
violent passions, whose sentiments are right, though
his actions are wrong; whose virtues are obscured by
negligence, and whose understanding is dissipated by
levity. In his idle hours he is rather loose than wicked,
and when the occasion forces out his latent qualities,
he is great without effort, and brave without tumult.
The trifler is roused into a hero, and the hero again
reposes in the trifler. This character is great, original,
and just.

Piercy is a rugged soldier, cholerick, and quarrelsome, and has only the soldier's virtues, generosity and courage.

But *Falstaff* unimitated, unimitable *Falstaff*, how shall I describe thee? Thou compound of sense and vice; of sense which may be admired but not esteemed, of vice which may be despised, but hardly detested. *Falstaff* is a character loaded with faults, and with those faults which naturally produce contempt. He is a thief, and a glutton, a coward, and a boaster, always ready to cheat the weak, and prey upon the poor; to terrify the timorous and insult the defenceless. At once obsequious and malignant, he satirises in their absence those whom he lives by flattering. He is familiar with the prince only as an agent of vice, but of this familiarity he is so proud as not only to be supercilious and haughty with common men, but to think his interest of importance to the duke of *Lancaster*. Yet the man thus corrupt, thus despicable, makes himself necessary to the prince that despises him, by the most pleasing of all qualities, perpetual gaiety, by an unfailing power of exciting laughter, which is the more freely indulged, as his wit is not of the splendid or ambitious kind, but consists in easy escapes and sallies of levity, which make sport but raise no envy. It must be observed that he is stained with no enormous or sanguinary crimes, so that his licentiousness is not so offensive but that it may be borne for his mirth.

The moral to be drawn from this representation is, that no man is more dangerous than he that with a will to corrupt, hath the power to please; and that neither wit nor honesty ought to think themselves safe with such a companion when they see *Henry* seduced by *Falstaff*.

THE LIFE OF KING HENRY V.

PROLOGUE. (CHORUS 3–4.)

> *A Kingdom for a stage, Princes to act,*
> *And Monarchs to behold the swelling scene!*

Shakespeare does not seem to set distance enough between the performers and spectators.

PROLOGUE. (CHORUS 12–14.)

> *May we cram*
> *Within this wooden O, the very caskes*
> *That did affright the air, at Agincourt?*

Nothing shews more evidently the power of custom over language, than that the frequent use of calling a circle an *O* could so much hide the meanness of the metaphor from *Shakespeare*, that he has used it many times where he makes his most eager attempts at dignity of stile.

PROLOGUE. (CHORUS 18.) *Imaginary forces.*

Imaginary for *imaginative*, or your powers of fancy. Active and passive words are by this authour frequently confounded.

PROLOGUE. (CHORUS 25.) *And make imaginary puissance.*

This passage shews that *Shakespeare* was fully sensible of the absurdity of shewing battles on the theatre, which indeed is never done but tragedy becomes farce. Nothing can be represented to the eye but by something like it, and *within a wooden O* nothing very like a battle can be exhibited.

ACT I. SCENE i. (1. i. 38.)

> *Hear him but reason in divinity.*

This scene was added after King *James*'s accession to the crown, so that we have no way of avoiding its being esteemed a compliment to *him*.—WARBURTON.

Why these lines should be divided from the rest of

the speech and applied to king *James*, I am not able
to conceive ; nor why an opportunity should be so
eagerly snatched to treat with contempt that part of
his character which was least contemptible. King
James's theological knowledge was not inconsiderable.
To preside at disputations is not very suitable to
a king, but to understand the questions is surely
laudable. The poet, if he had *James* in his thoughts,
was no skilful encomiast ; for the mention of *Harry*'s
skill in war, forced upon the remembrance of his
audience the great deficiency of their present king ;
who yet with all his faults, and many faults he had,
was such that Sir *Robert Cotton* says, *he would be
content that* England *should never have a better, provided
that it should never have a worse.*

ACT I. SCENE i. (I. i. 47–8.)
                              When he speaks,
          The air, a charter'd libertine, is still.

This line is exquisitely beautiful.

ACT II. SCENE iii. (II. ii. 126–7.)
   KING HENRY. *Oh, how hast thou with jealousy infected*
                    The sweetness of affiance.

Shakespeare urges this aggravation of the guilt of
treachery with great judgment. One of the worst
consequences of breach of trust is the diminution of
that confidence which makes the happiness of life, and
the dissemination of suspicion, which is the poison of
society.

ACT II. SCENE iii. (II. ii. 165.)
   GREY. *My fault, but not my body, pardon, Sovereign.*

One of the conspirators against Queen *Elizabeth*,
I think *Parry*, concludes his letter to her with these

words, a culpa, *but not* a pœna ; *absolve me most dear Lady.* This letter was much read at that time, and the authour doubtless copied it.

Act II. Scene iv. (ii. iii. 27-8.)   *Cold as any stone.*

Such is the end of *Falstaff,* from whom *Shakespeare* had promised us in his epilogue to *Henry* IV. that we should receive more entertainment. It happened to *Shakespeare* as to other writers, to have his imagination crowded with a tumultuary confusion of images, which, while they were yet unsorted and unexamined, seemed sufficient to furnish a long train of incidents, and a new variety of merriment, but which, when he was to produce them to view, shrunk suddenly from him, or could not be accommodated to his general design. That he once designed to have brought *Falstaff* on the scene again, we know from himself ; but whether he could contrive no train of adventures suitable to his character, or could match him with no companions likely to quicken his humour, or could open no new vein of pleasantry, and was afraid to continue the same strain lest it should not find the same reception, he has here for ever discarded him, and made haste to dispatch him, perhaps for the same reason for which *Addison* killed Sir *Roger,* that no other hand might attempt to exhibit him.

Let meaner authours learn from this example, that it is dangerous to sell the bear which is yet not hunted, to promise to the publick what they have not written.

This disappointment probably inclined Queen *Elizabeth* to command the poet to produce him once again, and to shew him in love or courtship. This was indeed a new source of humour, and produced a new play from the former characters.

I forgot to note in the proper place, and therefore note here, that *Falstaff*'s courtship, or *The Merry Wives of* Windsor, should be read between *Henry* IV. and *Henry* V.

ACT III. SCENE iii. (III. ii. 82 foll.)

It were to be wished that the poor merriment of this dialogue [between Macmorris and Captain Jamy] had not been purchased with so much profaneness.

ACT III. SCENE v. (III. iv.)

> CATHERINE. *Alice, tu as esté en Angleterre,* &c.

This scene is indeed mean enough, when it is read, but the grimaces of two *French* women, and the odd accent with which they uttered the *English*, made it divert upon the stage. It may be observed, that there is in it not only the *French* language, but the *French* spirit. *Alice* compliments the princess upon her knowledge of four words, and tells her that she pronounces like the *English* themselves. The princess suspects no deficiency in her instructress, nor the instructress in herself. Throughout the whole scene there may be found *French* servility, and *French* vanity.

ACT III. SCENE vi. (III. v. 40 foll.)

> *Charles Delabreth, high constable of* France, &c.

Milton somewhere bids the *English* take notice how their names are misspelt by foreigners, and seems to think that we may lawfully treat foreign names in return with the same neglect. This privilege seems to be exercised in this catalogue of *French* names, which, since the sense of the authour is not affected, I have left it as I found it.

ACT III. SCENE vi. (III. v. 50-2.)

> *Rush on his host, as doth the melted snow*
> *Upon the vallies ; whose low vassal seat*
> *The* Alps *doth spit and void his rheum upon.*

The poet has here defeated himself by passing too

soon from one image to another. To bid the *French* rush upon the *English* as the torrents formed from melted snow stream from the *Alps*, was at once vehement and proper, but its force is destroyed by the grossness of the thought in the next line.

ACT III. SCENE viii. (III. vi. 114-15.)
  FLUELLEN. *His nose is executed, and his fire's out.*

This is the last time that any sport can be made with the red face of *Bardolph*, which, to confess the truth, seems to have taken more hold on *Shakespeare*'s imagination than on any other. The conception is very cold to the solitary reader, though it may be somewhat invigorated by the exhibition on the stage. This poet is always more careful about the present than the future, about his audience than his readers.

ACT III. SCENE viii. (III. vi, 133-4.) *Now speak we on our cue.*

In our turn. This phrase the authour learned among players, and has imparted it to kings.

ACT IV. SCENE i. (IV. CHORUS 2-3.)
          The poring dark
  Fills the wide vessel of the universe.
We are not to think *Shakespear* so ignorant as to imagine it was night over the whole globe at once.—WARBURTON.

There is a better proof that *Shakespeare* knew the order of night and day in *Macbeth*.

      Now o'er one half the *world*
      Nature seems dead.

But there was no great need of any justification. The *universe*, in its original sense, no more means this globe singly than the circuit of the horizon; but, however large in its philosophical sense, it may be poetically used for as much of the world as falls under observation. Let me remark further, that ignorance cannot be certainly inferred from inaccuracy. Knowledge is not always present.

ACT IV. SCENE iv. (IV. i. 189-90.)

Every subject's duty is the King's, but every subject's soul is his own.

This is a very just distinction, and the whole argument is well followed, and properly concluded.

ACT IV. SCENE v. (IV. i. 250 foll.)

KING HENRY. *Upon the King!* &c.

There is something very striking and solemn in this soliloquy, into which the king breaks immediately as soon as he is left alone. Something like this, on less occasions, every breast has felt. Reflection and seriousness rush upon the mind upon the separation of a gay company, and especially after forced and unwilling merriment.

ACT IV. SCENE viii. (IV. iii. 24.)

KING HENRY. *By Jove, I am not covetous of gold.*

The king prays like a christian, and swears like a heathen.

ACT IV. SCENE viii. (IV. iii. 50-1.)

They'll remember, with advantages,
What feats they did that day.

Old men, notwithstanding the natural forgetfulness of age, shall remember *their feats of this day*, and remember to tell them *with advantage*. Age is commonly boastful, and inclined to magnify past acts and past times.

ACT IV. SCENE viii. (IV. iii. 57-9.)

Crispin Crispian shall ne'er go by,
From this day to the ending of the world,
But we in it shall be remembered.

It may be observed that we are apt to promise to

ourselves a more lasting memory than the changing state of human things admits. This prediction is not verified ; the feast of *Crispin* passes by without any mention of *Agincourt*. Late events obliterate the former : the civil wars have left in this nation scarcely any tradition of more ancient history.

Aᴄᴛ IV. Sᴄᴇɴᴇ ix. (ɪᴠ. iii. 104.)
> *Mark then abounding valour in our English.*

The *valour* of a putrid body, that destroys by the stench, is one of the thoughts that do no great honour to the poet. Perhaps from this putrid valour *Dryden* might borrow the posthumous empire of Don *Sebastian,* who was to reign wheresoever his atoms should be scattered.

Aᴄᴛ IV. Sᴄᴇɴᴇ xiv. (ɪᴠ. vii. 51-2.)
> *The fat Knight with the great belly-doublet.*

This is the last time that *Falstaff* can make sport. The poet was loath to part with him, and has continued his memory as long as he could.

Aᴄᴛ V. Sᴄᴇɴᴇ ii. (ᴠ. i. 94.)   *Exit* Pistol.

The comick scenes of the history of *Henry* the fourth and fifth are now at an end, and all the comick personages are now dismissed. *Falstaff* and Mrs. *Quickly* are dead ; *Nym* and *Bardolph* are hanged ; *Gadshill* was lost immediately after the robbery ; *Poins* and *Peto* have vanished since, one knows not how ; and *Pistol* is now beaten into obscurity. I believe every reader regrets their departure.

Aᴄᴛ V. Sᴄᴇɴᴇ iv. (ᴠ. ii. 125 foll.)
  Kɪɴɢ Hᴇɴʀʏ. *I'faith,* Kate, *thou wouldst find me such a plain* King, &c.

I know not why *Shakespeare* now gives the king nearly

such a character as he made him formerly ridicule in *Percy*. This military grossness and unskilfulness in all the softer arts, does not suit very well with the gaieties of his youth, with the general knowledge ascribed to him at his accession, or with the contemptuous message sent him by the *Dauphin*, who represents him as fitter for the ball room than the field, and tells him that he is not *to revel into dutchies*, or win provinces *with a nimble galliard*. The truth is, that the poet's matter failed him in the fifth act, and he was glad to fill it up with whatever he could get; and not even *Shakespeare* can write well without a proper subject. It is a vain endeavour for the most skilful hand to cultivate barrenness, or to paint upon vacuity.

Act V. Scene v. (v. ii. 305-402.)

We have here but a mean dialogue for princes; the merriment is very gross, and the sentiments are very worthless.

This play has many scenes of high dignity, and many of easy merriment. The character of the King is well supported, except in his courtship, where he has neither the vivacity of *Hal*, nor the grandeur of *Henry*. The humour of *Pistol* is very happily continued; his character has perhaps been the model of all the bullies that have yet appeared on the *English* stage.

The lines given to the chorus have many admirers; but the truth is, that in them a little may be praised, and much must be forgiven; nor can it be easily discovered why the intelligence given by the chorus is more necessary in this play than in many others where it is omitted. The great defect of this play is the emptiness and narrowness of the last act, which a very little diligence might have easily avoided.

THE FIRST PART OF KING HENRY VI.

Act I. Scene i. (i. i. 25, 27.)

> *The subtle-witted French*
> *By magick verse have thus contriv'd his end.*

There was a notion prevalent a long time, that life might be taken away by metrical charms. As superstition grew weaker these charms were imagined only to have power on irrational animals. In our authour's time it was supposed that the *Irish* could kill rats by a song.

Act II. Scene vi. (ii. v. 1–2.)

> Mortimer. *Kind keepers of my weak decaying age*
> *Let dying* Mortimer *here rest himself.*

I know not whether *Milton* did not take from this hint the lines with which he opens his tragedy.

Act III. Scene ix. (iii. iii. 85.)

> *Done like a* Frenchman : *turn, and turn again !*

The inconstancy of the *French* was always the subject of satire. I have read a dissertation written to prove that the index of the wind upon our steeples was made in form of a cock, to ridicule the *French* for their frequent changes.

Act IV. Scene vi. (iv. v.) Enter *Talbot* and his son.

For what reason this scene is written in rhyme I cannot guess. If *Shakespeare* had not in other plays mingled his rhymes and blank verses in the same manner, I should have suspected that this dialogue had been a part of some other poem which was never finished, and that being loath to throw his labour away, he inserted it here.

ACT V. SCENE i. (IV. VII.)

The return of rhyme where young *Talbot* is again mentioned, and in no other place, strengthens the suspicion, that these verses were originally part of some other work, and were copied here only to save the trouble of composing new.

ACT V. SCENE iii. (v. iii. 6.)   *Monarch of the North.*

The North was always supposed to be the particular habitation of bad spirits.   *Milton* therefore assembles the rebel angels in the North.

ACT V. SCENE iv. (v. iii. 62 foll.)
As plays the sun upon the glassy streams, &c.

This comparison, made between things which seem sufficiently unlike, is intended to express the softness and delicacy of Lady *Margaret*'s beauty, which delighted, but did not dazzle ; which was bright, but gave no pain by its lustre.

Of this play there is no copy earlier than that of the folio in 1623, though the two succeeding parts are extant in two editions in quarto.   That the second and third parts were published without the first may be admitted as no weak proof that the copies were surreptitiously obtained, and that the printers of that time gave the publick those plays not such as the authour designed, but such as they could get them.   That this play was written before the two others is indubitably collected from the series of events ;   that it was written and played before *Henry* the fifth is apparent, because in the epilogue there is mention made of this play and not of the other parts.

Henry *the sixth in swaddling bands crown'd king,*
Whose state so many had i'th' managing
That they lost France, *and made all* England *rue,*
Which oft our stage hath shewn.

France is lost in this play. The two following contain, as the old title imports, the contention of the houses of *York* and *Lancaster.*

The two first parts of *Henry* VI. were printed in 1600. When *Henry* V. was written we know not, but it was printed likewise in 1600, and therefore before the publication of the first and second parts, the first part of *Henry* VI. had been often *shown on the stage,* and would certainly have appeared in its place had the authour been the publisher.

THE SECOND PART OF KING HENRY VI.

It is apparent that this play begins where the former ends, and continues the series of transactions, of which it presupposes the first part already known. This is a sufficient proof that the second and third parts were not written without dependance on the first, though they were printed as containing a complete period of history.

Act II. Scene i. (II. i. 3-4.)

> *The wind was very high,*
> *And, ten to one, old* Joan *had not gone out.*

I am told by a gentleman better acquainted with falconry than myself, that the meaning, however expressed, is, that, the wind being high, it was ten to one that the old hawk had flown quite away; a trick which hawks often play their masters in windy weather.

Act II. Scene vii. (II. iv. 111.)

> Eleanor. *I long to see my prison.*

This impatience of a high spirit is very natural. It

is not so dreadful to be imprisoned, as it is desirable in a state of disgrace to be sheltered from the scorn of gazers.

Act III. Scene iii. (III. i. 210–11.)

> *And as the Butcher takes away the Calf,*
> *And binds the wretch, and beats it when it strays.*

I am inclined to believe that in this passage, as in many, there is a confusion of ideas, and that the poet had at once before him a butcher carrying a calf bound, and a butcher driving a calf to the slaughter, and beating him when he did not keep the path. Part of the line was suggested by one image and part by another, so that *strive* is the best word, but *stray* is the right.

Act III. Scene vi. (III. ii. 161–2.)

> *Oft have I seen a timely-parted ghost,*
> *Of ashy semblance, meager, pale, and bloodless.*

All that is true of the *body* of a dead man is here said by *Warwick* of the soul. I would read,

> *Oft have I seen a timely-parted* coarse,

But of two common words how or why was one changed for the other? I believe the transcriber thought that the epithet *timely-parted* could not be used of the body, but that, as in *Hamlet* there is mention of *peace-parted souls*, so here *timely-parted* must have the same substantive. He removed one imaginary difficulty and made many real. If the soul is parted from the body, the body is likewise parted from the soul.

I cannot but stop a moment to observe that this horrible description is scarcely the work of any pen but *Shakespeare*'s.

Act III. Scene viii. (III. ii. 310.)

> *Would curses kill, as doth the mandrake's groan.*

The fabulous accounts of the plant called a *mandrake*

give it an inferiour degree of animal life, and relate, that when it is torn from the ground, it groans, and that this groan being certainly fatal to him that is offering such unwelcome violence, the practice of those who gather mandrakes is to tie one end of a string to the plant, and the other to a dog, upon which the fatal groan discharges its malignity.

Act III. Scene viii. (III. ii. 333.)
You bad me ban, and will you bid me leave ?

This inconsistency is very common in real life. Those who are vexed to impatience are angry to see others less disturbed than themselves, but when others begin to rave, they themselves see in them, what they could not find in themselves, the deformity and folly of useless rage.

Act III. Scene x. (III. iii.)   *Death of Cardinal Beaufort.*

This is one of the scenes which have been applauded by the criticks, and which will continue to be admired when prejudice shall cease, and bigotry give way to impartial examination. These are beauties that rise out of nature and of truth ; the superficial reader cannot miss them, the profound can image nothing beyond them.

Act IV. Scene i. (IV. i. 1.)   *The gaudy, blabbing . . . day.*

The epithet *blabbing* applied to the day by a man about to commit murder, is exquisitely beautiful. Guilt is afraid of light, considers darkness as a natural shelter, and makes night the confidante of those actions which cannot be trusted to the *tell-tale day.*

Act IV. Scene i. (IV. i. 3-6.)
The jades
That drag the tragick melancholy night,
Who with their drowsy, slow, and flagging wings,
Clip dead mens' graves.

The *wings* of the *jades* that drag night appears an

unnatural image, till it is remembered that the chariot of the night is supposed, by *Shakespeare*, to be drawn by dragons.

ACT IV. SCENE ii. (IV. ii. 38.)

> CADE. *For our enemies shall fall before us.*

He alludes to his name *Cade*, from *cado*, Lat. *to fall*. He has too much learning for his character.

ACT IV. SCENE ii. (IV. ii. 81–2.) *There shall be no money.*

To mend the world by banishing money is an old contrivance of those who did not consider that the quarrels and mischiefs which arise from money, as the sign or ticket of riches, must, if money were to cease, arise immediately from riches themselves, and could never be at an end till every man was contented with his own share of the goods of life.

ACT IV. SCENE vi. (IV. vii. 39–40.)

> *Thou hast caused printing to be us'd.*

Shakespeare is a little too early with this accusation.

ACT IV. SCENE vi. (IV. vii. 54–5.)

> *Thou ought'st not to let thy horse wear a cloak.*

This is a reproach truly characteristical. Nothing gives so much offence to the lower ranks of mankind as the sight of superfluities merely ostentatious.

ACT IV. SCENE ix. (IV. x. 84.)

> *So wish I, I might thrust thy soul to hell.*

Not to dwell upon the wickedness of this horrid wish, with which *Iden* debases his character, this whole speech is wild and confused. To draw a man *by the heels, headlong*, is somewhat difficult ; nor can I discover how *the dunghill would be his grave* if *his trunk* were left *to be fed upon by crows*. These I conceive not to be the faults of corruption, but of negligence, and therefore do not attempt correction.

THE THIRD PART OF KING HENRY VI.

This play is only divided from the former for the convenience of exhibition ; for the series of action is continued without interruption, nor are any two scenes of any play more closely connected than the first scene of this play with the last of the former.

ACT I. SCENE iii. (I. i. 236.)

> *What is it but to make thy Sepulchre.*

The Queen's reproach is founded on a position long received among politicians, that the loss of a King's power is soon followed by loss of life.

ACT I. SCENE iv. (I. ii. 22–3.)

> *An oath is of no moment, being not took*
> *Before a true and lawful magistrate.*

The obligation of an oath is here eluded by very despicable sophistry. A lawful magistrate alone has the power to exact an oath, but the oath derives no part of its force from the magistrate. The plea against the obligation of an oath obliging to maintain an usurper, taken from the unlawfulness of the oath itself in the foregoing play, was rational and just.

ACT I. SCENE iv. (I. ii. 49–50.)

> *The Queen, with all the Northern Earls and Lords,*
> *Intend here to besiege you in your castle.*

I know not whether the authour intended any moral instruction, but he that reads this has a striking admonition against that precipitancy by which men often use unlawful means to do that which a little delay would put honestly in their power. Had *York* staid but a few moments he had saved his cause from the stain of perjury.

Act I. Scene vi. (I. iv. 132.)

'Tis government that makes them [i.e. women] seem divine.

Government, in the language of that time, signified evenness of temper, and decency of manners.

Act II. Scene i. (II. i. 48.)

EDWARD. *Oh, speak no more!*

The generous tenderness of *Edward,* and **savage** fortitude of *Richard,* are well distinguished by their different reception of their father's death.

Act II. Scene ii. (II. i. 130–2.)

Our soldiers, like the night-owl's lazy flight,
Or like a lazy thrasher with a flail,
Fell gently down.

This image [of the night-owl] is not very congruous to the subject, nor was it necessary to the comparison, which is happily enough completed by the thresher.

Act II. Scene vi. (II. v. 21 foll.)

O God! methinks it were a happy life
To be no better than a homely swain.

This speech is mournful and soft, exquisitely suited to the character of the king, and makes a pleasing interchange, by affording, amidst the tumult and horrour of the battle, an unexpected glimpse of rural innocence and pastoral tranquillity.

Act III. Scene i. (III. i. 17.) *Thy balm washt off.*

It is common in these plays to find the same images, whether jocular or serious, frequently recurring.

Act III. Scene ii. (III. ii. 16 foll.)

This is a very lively and spritely dialogue [between King Edward and Lady Gray]; the reciprocation is quicker than is common in *Shakespeare.*

ACT III. SCENE iii. (III. ii. 161.) *Unlick'd bear-whelp.*

It was an opinion which, in spite of its absurdity, prevailed long, that the bear brings forth only shapeless lumps of animated flesh, which she licks into the form of bears. It is now well known that the whelps of a bear are produced in the same state with those of other creatures.

ACT III. SCENE iii. (III. ii. 166–7.)

> *To o'erbear such*
> *As are of better person than myself.*

Richard speaks here the language of nature. Whoever is stigmatised with deformity has a constant source of envy in his mind, and would counterballance by some other superiority these advantages which they feel themselves to want. *Bacon* remarks that the deformed are commonly daring, and it is almost proverbially observed that they are ill-natured. The truth is, that the deformed, like all other men, are displeased with inferiority, and endeavour to gain ground by good or bad means, as they are virtuous or corrupt.

ACT III. SCENE v. (III. iii. 127.) *Exempt from envy.*

Envy is always supposed to have some fascinating or blasting power, and to be out of the reach of envy is therefore a privilege belonging only to great excellence.

ACT IV. SCENE i. (IV. i. 42–3.)

> HASTINGS. *'Tis better using France, than trusting France.*
>   *Let us be back'd with God, and with the seas.*

This has been the advice of every man who in any age understood and favoured the interest of *England.*

ACT IV. SCENE i. (IV. i. 56.)

> *You would not have bestow'd the heir.*

It must be remembered, that till the restoration the

heiresses of great estates were in the wardship of the king, who in their minority gave them up to plunder, and afterwards matched them to his favourites. I know not when liberty gained more than by the abolition of the court of wards.

Act IV. Scene vii. (IV. vi. 29.)

Few men rightly temper with the stars.

I suppose the meaning is, that few men conform their *temper* to their destiny, which King *Henry* did, when finding himself unfortunate he gave the management of publick affairs to more prosperous hands.

Act IV. Scene vii. (IV. vi. 70.)

This pretty lad will prove our country's bliss.

He was afterwards *Henry* VII. A man who put an end to the civil war of the two houses, but not otherwise remarkable for virtue. *Shakespeare* knew his trade. *Henry* VII. was Grandfather to Queen *Elizabeth*, and the King from whom *James* inherited.

Act V. Scene iii. (V. ii. 24–5.)

My parks, my walks, my manors that I had,
Ev'n now forsake me.

Cedes coëmptis saltibus, et domo, Villâque.   Hor.

This mention of his *parks* and *manours* diminishes the pathetick effect of the foregoing lines.

Act V. Scene vi. (V. iv. 67 foll.)

This scene is ill-contrived, in which the king and queen appear at once on the stage at the head of opposite armies. It had been easy to make one retire before the other entered.

Act V. Scene vi. (V. v. 51.)

Queen. *Oh* Ned, *sweet* Ned !

The condition of this warlike queen would move

compassion could it be forgotten that she gave *York*, to wipe his eyes in his captivity, a handkerchief stained with his young child's blood.

The three parts of *Henry* VI. are suspected, by Mr. *Theobald*, of being supposititious, and are declared, by Dr. *Warburton*, to be *certainly not Shakespeare's*. Mr. *Theobald's* suspicion arises from some obsolete words ; but the phraseology is like the rest of our authour's stile, and single words, of which however I do not observe more than two, can conclude little.

Dr. *Warburton* gives no reason, but I suppose him to judge upon deeper principles and more comprehensive views, and to draw his opinion from the general effect and spirit of the composition, which he thinks inferior to the other historical plays.

From mere inferiority nothing can be inferred ; in the productions of wit there will be inequality. Sometimes judgment will err, and sometimes the matter itself will defeat the artist. Of every authour's works one will be the best, and one will be the worst. The colours are not equally pleasing, nor the attitudes equally graceful, in all the pictures of *Titian* or *Reynolds*.

Dissimilitude of stile and heterogeneousness of sentiment, may sufficiently show that a work does not really belong to the reputed authour. But in these plays no such marks of spuriousness are found. The diction, the versification, and the figures, are *Shakespeare's*. These plays, considered, without regard to characters and incidents, merely as narratives in verse, are more happily conceived and more accurately finished than those of king *John*, *Richard* II., or the tragick scenes of *Henry* IV. and V. If we take these plays from *Shakespeare*, to whom shall they be given? What authour of that age had the same easiness of expression and fluency of numbers?

Having considered the evidence given by the plays themselves, and found it in their favour, let us now enquire what corroboration can be gained from other testimony. They are ascribed to *Shakespeare* by the first editors, whose attestation may be received in questions of fact, however unskilfully they superintended their edition. They seem to be declared genuine by the voice of *Shakespeare* himself, who refers to the second play in his epilogue to *Henry* V. and apparently connects the first act of *Richard* III. with the last of the third part of *Henry* VI. If it be objected that the plays were popular, and therefore he alluded to them as well known ; it may be answered, with equal probability, that the natural passions of a poet would have disposed him to separate his own works from those of an inferior hand. And indeed if an authour's own testimony is to be overthrown by speculative criticism, no man can be any longer secure of literary reputation.

Of these three plays I think the second the best. The truth is, that they have not sufficient variety of action, for the incidents are too often of the same kind ; yet many of the characters are well discriminated. King *Henry*, and his queen, king *Edward*, the duke of *Gloucester*, and the earl of *Warwick*, are very strongly and distinctly painted.

The old copies of the two latter parts of *Henry* VI. and of *Henry* V. are so apparently imperfect and mutilated, that there is no reason for supposing them the first draughts of *Shakespeare*. I am inclined to believe them copies taken by some auditor who wrote down, during the representation, what the time would permit, then perhaps filled up some of his omissions at a second or third hearing, and when he had by this method formed something like a play, sent it to the printer.

THE LIFE AND DEATH OF KING RICHARD III.

Act I. Scene i. (i. i. 28.)

And therefore, since I cannot prove a lover.

Shakespeare very diligently inculcates, that the wickedness of *Richard* proceeded from his deformity, from the envy that rose at the comparison of his own person with others, and which incited him to disturb the pleasures that he could not partake.

Act I. Scene i. (i. i. 108–10.)

Gloucester. *Whatsoe'er you will employ me in,*
Were it to call King Edward's widow sister,
I will perform it.

This is a very covert and subtle manner of insinuating treason. The natural expression would have been, *were it to call King Edward's wife sister.* I will solicit for you though it should be at the expence of so much degradation and constraint, as to own the lowborn wife of King *Edward* for a sister. But by slipping as it were casually *widow* into the place of *wife*, he tempts *Clarence* with an oblique proposal to kill the king.

Act I. Scene ii. (i. ii. 55–6.)

See, dead Henry's *wounds*
Open their congeal'd mouths and bleed afresh.

It is a tradition very generally received, that the murdered body bleeds on the touch of the murderer. This was so much believed by Sir *Kenelm Digby* that he has endeavoured to explain the reason.

Act I. Scene ii. (i. ii. 153.) *They kill me with a living death.*

In imitation of this passage, and I suppose of a thousand more ;

——— *a living death I bear,*
Says Dapperwit, and sunk beside his chair.

Act I. Scene ii. (I. ii. 180–1.)
> *I did kill King* Henry,
> *But 'twas thy beauty that provoked me.*

Shakespeare countenances the observation, that no woman can ever be offended with the mention of her beauty.

Act I. Scene iv. (I. iii. 242.) *Bottled spider.*

A *spider* is called bottled, because, like other insects, he has a middle slender and a belly protuberant. *Richard's* form and venom make her liken him to a spider.

Act II. Scene i. (II. i. 103.)
> *Have I a tongue to doom my brother's death.*

This lamentation is very tender and pathetic. The recollection of the good qualities of the dead is very natural, and no less naturally does the king endeavour to communicate the crime to others.

Act IV. Scene i. (IV. i. 84.) *But with his tim'rous dreams.*

'Tis recorded by *Polydore Virgil*, that *Richard* was frequently disturbed by terrible dreams : this is therefore no fiction.

Act IV. Scene ii. (IV. ii. 94 foll.)

The allusions to the plays of *Henry* VI. are no weak proofs of the authenticity of these disputed pieces.

Act IV. Scene v. (IV. iv. 199 foll.) *Stay, Madam.*

On this dialogue [between Richard and the Queen] 'tis not necessary to bestow much criticism : part of it is ridiculous, and the whole improbable.

Act V. Scene v. (V. iii. 178 foll.) *Give me another horse.*

There is in this, as in many of our authour's speeches

of passion, something very trifling, and something very striking. *Richard*'s debate, whether he should quarrel with himself, is too long continued, but the subsequent exaggeration of his crimes is truly tragical.

This is one of the most celebrated of our authour's performances; yet I know not whether it has not happened to him as to others, to be praised most when praise is not most deserved. That this play has scenes noble in themselves, and very well contrived to strike in the exhibition, cannot be denied. But some parts are trifling, others shocking, and some improbable.

THE LIFE OF KING HENRY VIII.

PROLOGUE.

This is not the only passage in which *Shakespeare* has discovered his conviction of the impropriety of battles represented on the stage. He knew that five or six men with swords give a very unsatisfactory idea of an army, and therefore, without much care to excuse his former practice, he allows that a theatrical fight would destroy all *opinion* of *truth*, and *leave* him *never an understanding friend. Magnis ingeniis et multa nihilominus habituris simplex convenit erroris confessio.* Yet I know not whether the coronation shewn in this play may not be liable to all that can be objected against a battle.

ACT I. SCENE i. (I. i. 15–16.)

> *Till this time Pomp was single, but now marry'd*
> *To one above itself.*

Dr. *Warburton* has here discovered more beauty than the authour intended, who meant only to say in a noisy periphrasis, that *pomp was encreased on this occasion to more than twice as much as it had ever been before.* Pomp is no more married to the *English* than to the *French* king, for to neither is any preference given by the speaker. Pomp is only married to pomp, but the new pomp is greater than the old.

ACT I. SCENE ii. (I. i. 122-3.)

> *A beggar's book*
> *Out-worths a noble's blood.*

That is, the literary qualifications of a bookish beggar are more prized than the high descent of hereditary greatness. This is a contemptuous exclamation very naturally put into the mouth of one of the antient, unlettered, martial nobility.

ACT I. SCENE iv. (I. ii. 1-2.)

> KING. *My life itself, and the best heart of it,*
> *Thanks you for this great care.*

The expression is monstrous. The heart is supposed the seat of life : But, as if he had many lives, and to each of them, a heart, he says, *his best heart.* A way of speaking that would have become a cat rather than a King.—WARBURTON.

This expression is not more monstrous than many others. Heart is not here taken for the great organ of circulation and life, but, in a common and popular sense, for the most valuable or precious part. Our authour, in *Hamlet*, mentions the *heart of heart.* Exhausted and effete ground is said by the farmer to be *out of heart.* The hard and inner part of the oak is called *heart of oak.*

ACT I. SCENE iv. (I. ii. 32.) *The many to them 'longing.*

The *many* is the *meiny*, the train, the people. *Dryden* is, perhaps, the last that used this word.

> *The Kings before their many rode.*

Act I. Scene iv. (I. ii. 34-5.)

> *Compell'd by hunger*
> *And lack of other means.*

Means does not signify methods of livelihood, for that **was** said immediately before—*unfit for other life*; but it signifies, *necessaries*—*compelled*, says the speaker, *for want of bread and other necessaries.* But the poet using, for the thing, [*want of bread*] the effect of it, [*hunger*] the passage is become doubly obscure; first, by using a term in a licentious sense, and then by putting it to a vicious construction. The not apprehending that this is one of the distinguishing peculiarities in *Shakespear*'s stile, has been the occasion of so much ridiculous correction of him.—War-burton.

I have inserted this note rather because it seems to have been the writer's favourite, than because it is of much value. It explains what no reader has found difficult, and, I think, explains it wrong.

Act III. Scene i. (III. i. 103.)

> *Cardinal sins, and hollow hearts, I fear you.*

The distress of *Catharine* might have kept her from the quibble to which she is irresistibly tempted by the word *Cardinal*.

Act IV. Scene i. (IV. i. 9-10.)

> *They're ever forward*
> *In celebration of this day.*

Hanmer reads, *these days*, but *Shakespeare* meant *such a day as this*, a coronation day. And such is the *English* idiom, which our authour commonly prefers to grammatical nicety.

Act IV. Scene ii. (IV. ii.)

Enter *Catherine* Dowager, sick, led between *Griffith* her gentleman usher, and *Patience* her woman.

This scene is, above any other part of *Shakespeare*'s tragedies, and perhaps above any scene of any other poet, tender and pathetick, without gods, or furies, or poisons, or precipices, without the help of romantick circumstances, without improbable sallies of poetical lamentation, and without any throes of tumultuous misery.

Act V. Scene v. (v. iii. 10-12.)

> We are all men
> In our own natures frail, and capable
> Of frailty.

This sentence I think needed no commentary. The meaning, and the plain meaning, is, *we are men frail by nature, and therefore liable to acts of frailty*, to deviations from the right. I wish every commentator, before he suffers his confidence to kindle, would repeat,

> ———We are all men
> In our own natures frail, and capable
> Of frailty ; few are angels.

Act V. Scene vii. (v. iv. 23.)   *Sir* Guy, *nor* Colebrand.

Of *Guy* of *Warwick* every one has heard. *Colebrand* was the *Danish* giant whom *Guy* subdued at *Winchester*. Their combat is very elaborately described by *Drayton* in his *Polyolbion*.

Act V. Scene viii. (v. v. 40-56.)

> Nor shall this peace sleep with her, &c.

These lines, to the interruption by the King, seem to have been inserted at some revisal of the play after the accession of King *James*. If the passage, included in crochets, be left out, the speech of *Cranmer* proceeds in a regular tenour of prediction and continuity of sentiments ; but by the interposition of the new lines, he first celebrates *Elizabeth*'s successor, and then wishes he did not know that she was to die ; first rejoices at the consequence, and then laments the cause. Our authour was at once politick and idle ;

he resolved to flatter *James*, but neglected to reduce the whole speech to propriety, or perhaps intended that the lines inserted should be spoken in the action, and omitted in the publication, if any publication ever was in his thoughts. Mr. *Theobald* has made the same observation.

The play of *Henry* the eighth is one of those which still keeps possession of the stage, by the splendour of its pageantry. The coronation about forty years ago drew the people together in multitudes for a great part of the winter. Yet pomp is not the only merit of this play. The meek sorrows and virtuous distress of *Catherine* have furnished some scenes which may be justly numbered among the greatest efforts of tragedy. But the genius of *Shakespeare* comes in and goes out with *Catherine*. Every other part may be easily conceived, and easily written.

Though it is very difficult to decide whether short pieces be genuine or spurious, yet I cannot restrain myself from expressing my suspicion that neither the prologue nor epilogue to this play is the work *of Shakespeare ; non vultus, non color.* It appears to me very likely that they were supplied by the friendship or officiousness of *Johnson*, whose manner they will be perhaps found exactly to resemble. There is yet another supposition possible : the prologue and epilogue may have been written after *Shakespeare*'s departure from the stage, upon some accidental revisal of the play, and there will then be reason for imagining that the writer, whoever he was, intended no great kindness to him, this play being recommended by a subtle and covert censure of his other works. There is in *Shakespeare* so much of *fool and fight,*

——— *the fellow*
In a long motley coat, guarded with yellow,

appears so often in his drama, that I think it not very likely that he would have animadverted so severely on himself. All this, however, must be received as very dubious, since we know not the exact date of this or the other plays, and cannot tell how our authour might have changed his practice or opinions.

The historical Dramas are now concluded, of which the two parts of *Henry* the Fourth, and *Henry* the Fifth, are among the happiest of our authour's compositions; and King *John, Richard* the Third, and *Henry* the Eighth, deservedly stand in the second class. Those whose curiosity would refer the historical scenes to their original, may consult *Hollingshead*, and sometimes *Hall*: from *Hollingshead Shakespeare* has often inserted whole speeches with no more alteration than was necessary to the numbers of his verse. To transcribe them into the margin was unnecessary, because the original is easily examined, and they are seldom less perspicuous in the poet than in the historian.

To play histories, or to exhibit a succession of events by action and dialogue, was a common entertainment among our rude ancestors upon great festivities. The parish clerks once performed at *Clerkenwell* a play which lasted three days, containing, *The History of the World.*

KING LEAR.

Act I. Scene i. (i. i. 3-4.)   *In the division of the kingdom.*

There is something of obscurity or inaccuracy in this preparatory scene. The King has already divided his kingdom, and yet when he enters he examines his daughters, to discover in what proportions he should divide it. Perhaps *Kent* and *Gloucester* only were privy to his design, which he still kept in his own hands, to be changed or performed as subsequent reasons should determine him.

Act I. Scene ii. (i. i. 149 foll.)
Think'st thou, that duty shall have dread to speak, &c.

I have given this passage according to the old folio from which the modern editions have silently departed, for the sake of better numbers, with a degree of insincerity, which, if not sometimes detected and censured, must impair the credit of antient books. One of the editors, and perhaps only one, knew how much mischief may be done by such clandestine alterations.

The quarto agrees with the folio, except that for *reserve thy state*, it gives, *reverse thy doom*, and has *stoops* instead of *falls to folly*.

The meaning of *answer my life my judgment* is, *Let my life be answerable for my judgment*, or *I will stake my life on my opinion*.

The reading which, without any right, has possessed all the modern copies is this,

——— *to plainness Honour*
Is bound, when Majesty to folly falls.
Reserve thy state ; with better judgment check
This hideous rashness ; with my life I answer,
Thy youngest daughter, &c.

I am inclined to think that *reverse thy doom* was *Shakespeare*'s first reading, as more apposite to the present occasion, and that he changed it afterwards to *reserve thy state*, which conduces more to the progress of the action.

ACT I. SCENE ii. (I. i. 174-5.)

> *Which nor our nature, nor our place can bear,*
> *Our potency made good.*

Lear, who is characterized as hot, heady and violent, is, with very just observation of life, made to entangle himself with vows, upon any sudden provocation to vow revenge, and then to plead the obligation of a vow in defence of implacability.

ACT I SCENE ii. (I. i. 181.) *By* Jupiter.

Shakespeare makes his *Lear* too much a mythologist : he had *Hecate* and *Apollo* before.

ACT I. SCENE viii. (I. ii. 132 foll.)

EDMUND. *This is the excellent foppery of the world,* &c.

In *Shakespeare*'s best plays, besides the vices that arise from the subject, there is generally some peculiar prevailing folly, principally ridiculed, that runs thro' the whole piece. Thus, in the *Tempest*, the lying disposition of travellers, and in *As you like it*, the fantastick humour of courtiers, is exposed and satirised with infinite pleasantry. In like manner, in his play of *Lear*, the dotages of judicial astrology are severely ridiculed. I fancy, was the date of its first performance well considered, it would be found that something or other happened at that time which gave a more than ordinary run to this deceit, as these words seem to intimate, *I am thinking, brother, of a prediction I read this other day, what should follow these eclipses.* However this be, an impious cheat, which had so little

foundation in nature or reason, so detestable an
original, and such fatal consequences on the manners
of the people, who were at that time strangely besotted
with it, certainly deserved the severest lash of satire.
It was a fundamental in this noble science, that whatever seeds of good dispositions the infant unborn
might be endowed with, either from nature, or
traductively from its parents, yet if, at the time of
its birth, the delivery was by any casualty so accelerated
or retarded, as to fall in with the predominancy of
a malignant constellation, that momentary influence
would entirely change its nature, and bias it to all the
contrary ill qualities. So wretched and monstrous an
opinion did it set out with. But the *Italians*, to whom
we owe this, as well as most other unnatural crimes and
follies of these latter ages, fomented its original impiety
to the most detestable height of extravagance. *Petrus
Aponensis*, an *Italian* physician of the XIIIth century,
assures us that those prayers which are made to God
when the moon is in conjunction with *Jupiter* in the
Dragon's tail, are infallibly heard. The great *Milton*
with a just indignation of this impiety, hath, in his
Paradise Regained, satirized it in a very beautiful
manner, by putting these reveries into the mouth of
the Devil. Nor could the licentious *Rabelais* himself
forbear to ridicule this impious dotage, which he does
with exquisite address and humour, where, in the fable
which he so agreeably tells from *Æsop*, of the man who
applied to *Jupiter* for the loss of his hatchet, he makes
those, who, on the poor man's good success, had
projected to trick *Jupiter* by the same petition, a kind
of astrologick atheists, who ascribed this good fortune,
that they imagined they were now all going to partake
of, to the influence of some rare conjunction and con-
figuration of the stars. *Hen, hen, disent ils—Et
doncques, telle est au temps present la revolution des Cieulx,*

*la constellation des Astres, & aspect des Planetes, que
quiconque Coignée perdra, soubdain deviendra ainsi riche?*
——Nou. Prol. du IV. Livre.

But to return to *Shakespear*. So blasphemous a
delusion, therefore, it became the honesty of our poet
to expose. But it was a tender point, and required
managing. For this impious juggle had in his time
a kind of religious reverence paid to it. It was therefore to be done obliquely ; and the circumstances of
the scene furnished him with as good an opportunity
as he could wish. The persons in the drama are all
pagans, so that as, in compliance to custom, his good
characters were not to speak ill of judicial Astrology,
they could on account of their religion give no reputation to it. But in order to expose it the more, he,
with great judgment, makes these pagans Fatalists ; as
appears by these words of *Lear*,

> *By all the operations of the orbs,*
> *From whom we do exist and cease to be.*

For the doctrine of fate is the true foundation of
judicial Astrology. Having thus discredited it by the
very commendations given to it, he was in no danger
of having his direct satire against it mistaken, by its
being put (as he was obliged, both in paying regard
to custom, and in following nature) into the mouth
of the villain and atheist, especially when he has added
such force of reason to his ridicule, in the words
referred to in the beginning of the note.

ACT III. SCENE ix. (III. vi. 20-1.)
He's mad that trusts in the tameness of a wolf, a horse's health, &c.

Shakespeare is here speaking not of things maliciously
treacherous, but of things uncertain and not durable.
A horse is above all other animals subject to diseases.

Act IV. Scene i. (IV. i. 68–9.)

> Let the superfluous and lust-dieted man,
> That slaves your ordinance.

The language of *Shakespeare* is very licentious, and his words have often meanings remote from the proper and original use. To *slave* or *beslave* another is to *treat* him *with terms of indignity*; in a kindred sense, to *slave the ordinance*, may be, *to* slight *or* ridicule *it*.

Act IV. Scene v. (IV. v. 22.)

> REGAN. *Let me unseal the letter.*

I know not well why *Shakespeare* gives the Steward, who is a mere factor of wickedness, so much fidelity. He now refuses the letter, and afterwards, when he is dying, thinks only how it may be safely delivered.

Act IV. Scene vi. (IV. vi.) Enter *Glo'ster* and *Edgar*.

This scene and the stratagem by which *Glo'ster* is cured of his desperation, are wholly borrowed from *Sidney*'s *Arcadia*.

Act IV. Scene vi. (IV. vi. 12 foll.)

> *How fearful*
> *And dizzy 'tis, to cast one's eyes so low!*

This description has been much admired since the time of *Addison*, who has remarked, with a poor attempt at pleasantry, that *he who can read it without being giddy has a very good head, or a very bad one*. The description is certainly not mean, but I am far from thinking it wrought to the utmost excellence of poetry. He that looks from a precipice finds himself assailed by one great and dreadful image of irresistible destruction. But this overwhelming idea is dissipated and enfeebled from the instant that the mind can restore itself to the observation of particulars, and diffuse its attention to distinct objects. The enumeration of the choughs and crows, the samphire-man and the fishers, counteracts the great effect of the prospect, as it peoples the desert of intermediate vacuity, and stops the mind in the rapidity of its descent through emptiness and horrour.

ACT IV. SCENE vi. (IV. vi. 81.)

Bear free and patient thoughts.

To be melancholy is to have the mind *chained down* to one painful idea, there is therefore great propriety in exhorting *Glo'ster* to *free thoughts,* to an emancipation of his soul from grief and despair.

ACT IV. SCENE vii. (IV. vi. 8–9.)

That fellow handles his Bow like a Crow-keeper.

This *crow-keeper* was so common in the authour's time, that it is one of the few peculiarities mentioned by *Ortelius* in his account of our island.

ACT V. SCENE viii. (V. iii. 168.)

EDGAR. *Let's exchange charity.*

Our authour by negligence gives his heathens the sentiments and practices of christianity. In *Hamlet* there is the same solemn act of final reconciliation, but with exact propriety, for the personages are Christians.

Exchange forgiveness with me, noble Hamlet, &c.

The Tragedy of *Lear* is deservedly celebrated among the dramas of *Shakespeare.* There is perhaps no play which keeps the attention so strongly fixed ; which so much agitates our passions and interests our curiosity. The artful involutions of distinct interests, the striking opposition of contrary characters, the sudden changes of fortune, and the quick succession of events, fill the mind with a perpetual tumult of indignation, pity, and

hope.   There is no scene which does not contribute
to the aggravation of the distress or conduct of the
action, and scarce a line which does not conduce to
the progress of the scene.   So powerful is the current
of the poet's imagination, that the mind, which once
ventures within it, is hurried irresistibly along.

On the seeming improbability of *Lear*'s conduct it
may be observed, that he is represented according to
histories at that time vulgarly received as true.   And
perhaps if we turn our thoughts upon the barbarity
and ignorance of the age to which this story is referred,
it will appear not so unlikely as while we estimate *Lear*'s
manners by our own.   Such preference of one daughter
to another, or resignation of dominion on such con-
ditions, would be yet credible, if told of a petty prince
of *Guinea* or *Madagascar*.   *Shakespeare*, indeed, by the
mention of his Earls and Dukes, has given us the idea
of times more civilised, and of life regulated by softer
manners ;   and the truth is, that though he so nicely
discriminates, and so minutely describes the characters
of men, he commonly neglects and confounds the
characters of ages, by mingling customs ancient and
modern, *English* and foreign.

My learned friend Mr. *Warton*, who has in the
Adventurer very minutely criticised this play, remarks,
that the instances of cruelty are too savage and shocking, and that the intervention of *Edmund* destroys the
simplicity of the story.   These objections may, I think,
be answered, by repeating, that the cruelty of the
daughters is an historical fact, to which the poet has
added little, having only drawn it into a series by
dialogue and action.   But I am not able to apologise
with equal plausibility for the extrusion of *Gloucester*'s
eyes, which seems an act too horrid to be endured in
dramatick exhibition, and such as must always compel
the mind to relieve its distress by incredulity.   Yet

let it be remembered that our authour well knew what would please the audience for which he wrote.

The injury done by *Edmund* to the simplicity of the action is abundantly recompensed by the addition of variety, by the art with which he is made to co-operate with the chief design, and the opportunity which he gives the poet of combining perfidy with perfidy, and connecting the wicked son with the wicked daughters, to impress this important moral, that villany is never at a stop, that crimes lead to crimes, and at last terminate in ruin.

But though this moral be incidentally enforced, *Shakespeare* has suffered the virtue of *Cordelia* to perish in a just cause, contrary to the natural ideas of justice, to the hope of the reader, and, what is yet more strange, to the faith of chronicles. Yet this conduct is justified by the Spectator, who blames *Tate* for giving *Cordelia* success and happiness in his alteration, and declares, that, in his opinion, *the tragedy has lost half its beauty.* *Dennis* has remarked, whether justly or not, that, to secure the favourable reception of *Cato, the town was poisoned with much false and abominable criticism,* and that endeavours had been used to discredit and decry poetical justice. A play in which the wicked prosper, and the virtuous miscarry, may doubtless be good, because it is a just representation of the common events of human life : but since all reasonable beings naturally love justice, I cannot easily be persuaded, that the observation of justice makes a play worse ; or, that if other excellencies are equal, the audience will not always rise better pleased from the final triumph of persecuted virtue.

In the present case the publick has decided. *Cordelia,* from the time of *Tate,* has always retired with victory and felicity. And, if my sensations could add any thing to the general suffrage, I might relate, that I was

many years ago so shocked by *Cordelia*'s death, that
I know not whether I ever endured to read again the
last scenes of the play till I undertook to revise them
as an editor.

There is another controversy among the criticks
concerning this play. It is disputed whether the
predominant image in *Lear*'s disordered mind be the
loss of his kingdom or the cruelty of his daughters.
Mr. *Murphy*, a very judicious critick, has evinced by
induction of particular passages, that the cruelty of his
daughters is the primary source of his distress, and that
the loss of royalty affects him only as a secondary and
subordinate evil; He observes with great justness,
that *Lear* would move our compassion but little, did
we not rather consider the injured father than the
degraded king.

The story of this play, except the episode of *Edmund*,
which is derived, I think, from *Sidney*, is taken originally
from *Geoffry* of *Monmouth*, whom *Hollingshead* generally copied; but perhaps immediately from an old
historical ballad, of which I shall insert the greater part.
My reason for believing that the play was posteriour
to the ballad rather than the ballad to the play, is, that
the ballad has nothing of *Shakespeare*'s nocturnal tempest, which is too striking to have been omitted, and
that it follows the chronicle; it has the rudiments of
the play, but none of its amplifications: it first hinted
Lear's madness, but did not array it in circumstances.
The writer of the ballad added something to the
history, which is a proof that he would have added
more, if more had occurred to his mind, and more must
have occurred if he had seen *Shakespeare*.

TIMON OF ATHENS.

ACT I. SCENE i. (I. i. 21 foll.) *Our Poesy is as a Gum, &c.*

This speech of the poet is very obscure. He seems
to boast the copiousness and facility of his vein, by
declaring that verses drop from a poet as gums from
odoriferous trees, and that his flame kindles itself
without the violence necessary to elicite sparkles from
the flint. What follows next? that it, *like a current,
flies each bound it chafes.* This may mean, that it
expands itself notwithstanding all obstructions : but
the images in the comparison are so ill sorted, and the
effect so obscurely expressed, that I cannot but think
something omitted that connected the last sentence
with the former. It is well known that the players
often shorten speeches to quicken the representation ;
and it may be suspected, that they sometimes performed their amputations with more haste than
judgment.

ACT I. SCENE ii. (I. i. 108-9.)
> '*Tis not enough to help the feeble up,*
> *But to support him after.*

This thought is better expressed by Dr. *Madden* in
his elegy on Archbishop *Boulter.*

> ——*He thought it mean*
> *Only to help the poor to beg again.*

ACT III. SCENE iii. (III. iii. 33-4.)
Those that under hot, ardent, zeal would set whole Realms on fire.

This is a reflection on the Puritans of that time.
These people were then set upon a project of new-
modelling the ecclesiastical and civil government
according to scripture rules and examples. Which

makes him say, that *under zeal* for the word of God, they *would set whole realms on fire*.

ACT III. SCENE iv. (III. iv. 67.)   *Enter* Servilius.

It may be observed that *Shakespeare* has unskilfully filled his *Greek* story with *Roman* names.

ACT IV. SCENE ii. (IV. ii.)   *Enter* Flavius.

Nothing contributes more to the exaltation of *Timon's* character than the zeal and fidelity of his servants. Nothing but real virtue can be honoured by domesticks ; nothing but impartial kindness can gain affection from dependants.

ACT IV. SCENE v.

I cannot concur to censure *Theobald* as a *critick* very *unhappy*. He was weak, but he was cautious : finding but little power in his mind, he rarely ventured far under its conduct. This timidity hindered him from daring conjectures, and sometimes hindered him happily.

ACT IV. SCENE vi. (IV. iii. 253 foll.)   *Hadst thou, like us.*

There is in this speech a sullen haughtiness, and malignant dignity, suitable at once to the lord and the manhater. The impatience with which he bears to have his luxury reproached by one that never had luxury within his reach, is natural and graceful.

There is in a letter written by the earl of *Essex*, just before his execution, to another nobleman, a passage somewhat resembling this, with which I believe every reader will be pleased, though it is so serious and solemn that it can scarcely be inserted without irreverence.

" God grant your lordship may quickly feel the comfort I now enjoy in my unfeigned conversion, but that you may never feel the torments I have suffered for my long delaying it. *I had none but deceivers to call upon me, to whom I said, if my ambition could have entered into their narrow breasts, they would not have been so humble ; or if my delights had been once tasted by them, they would not have been so precise. But your lordship hath one to call upon you, that knoweth what it is you now enjoy ; and what the greatest fruit and end is of all contentment that this world can afford.* Think therefore, dear earl, that I have staked and buoyed all the ways of pleasure unto you, and left them as sea-marks for you to keep the channel of religious virtue. For shut your eyes never so long, they must be open at the last, and then you must say with me, *there is no peace to the ungodly.*"

ACT IV. SCENE vi. (IV. iii. 276–7.)

> *If thou hadst not been born the worst of men,*
> *Thou hadst been knave and flatterer.*

Dryden has quoted two verses of *Virgil* to shew how well he could have written satires. *Shakespeare* has here given a specimen of the same power by a line bitter beyond all bitterness, in which *Timon* tells *Apemantus*, that he had not virtue enough for the vices which he condemns.

ACT V. SCENE v. (V. iii. 6.)

There is something elaborately unskilful in the contrivance of sending a soldier, who cannot read, to take the epitaph in wax, only that it may close the play by being read with more solemnity in the last scene.

The play of *Timon* is a domestick Tragedy, and therefore strongly fastens on the attention of the reader. In the plan there is not much art, but the incidents are natural, and the characters various and exact. The catastrophe affords a very powerful warning against that ostentatious liberality, which scatters bounty, but confers no benefits, and buys flattery, but not friendship.

In this Tragedy are many passages perplexed, obscure, and probably corrupt, which I have endeavoured to rectify or explain with due diligence ; but having only one copy, cannot promise myself that my endeavours will be much applauded.

TITUS ANDRONICUS.

All the editors and criticks agree with Mr. *Theobald* in supposing this play spurious. I see no reason for differing from them ; for the colour of the stile is wholly different from that of the other plays, and there is an attempt at regular versification, and artificial closes, not always inelegant, yet seldom pleasing. The barbarity of the spectacles, and the general massacre which are here exhibited, can scarcely be conceived tolerable to any audience ; yet we are told by *Johnson*, that they were not only born but praised. That *Shakespeare* wrote any part, though *Theobald* declares it *incontestable*, I see no reason for believing.

The chronology of this play does not prove it not to be *Shakespeare*'s. If it had been written twenty-five years, in 1614, it might have been written when *Shakespeare* was twenty-five years old. When he left *Warwickshire* I know not, but at the age of twenty-five it was rather too late to fly for deer-stealing.

Ravenscroft, who, in the reign of *Charles* II. revised this play, and restored it to the stage, tells us in his preface, from a theatrical tradition I suppose, which in his time might be of sufficient authority, that this play was touched in different parts by *Shakespeare*, but written by some other poet. I do not find *Shakespeare*'s touches very discernible.

MACBETH.

Act I. Scene i. (I. i.) *Enter three Witches.*

In order to make a true estimate of the abilities and
merit of a writer, it is always necessary to examine the
genius of his age, and the opinions of his contemporaries. A poet who should now make the whole action
of his tragedy depend upon enchantment, and produce
the chief events by the assistance of supernatural
agents, would be censured as transgressing the bounds
of probability, be banished from the Theatre to the
nursery, and condemned to write fairy tales instead of
tragedies ; but a survey of the notions that prevailed
at the time when this play was written, will prove that
Shakespeare was in no danger of such censures, since
he only turned the system that was then universally
admitted to his advantage, and was far from over-
burthening the credulity of his audience.

The reality of witchcraft or enchantment, which,
though not strictly the same, are confounded in this
play, has in all ages and countries been credited by
the common people, and in most by the learned themselves. These phantoms have indeed appeared more
frequently, in proportion as the darkness of ignorance
has been more gross ; but it cannot be shown, that the
brightest gleams of knowledge have at any time been
sufficient to drive them out of the world. The time
in which this kind of credulity was at its height, seems
to have been that of the holy war, in which the
christians imputed all their defeats to enchantments
or diabolical opposition, as they ascribed their success
to the assistance of their military saints ; and the
learned Dr. *Warburton* appears to believe (*Suppl. to the
Introduction to Don* Quixote) that the first accounts
of enchantments were brought into this part of the
world by those who returned from their eastern

expeditions. But there is always some distance between the birth and maturity of folly as of wickedness : this opinion had long existed, though perhaps the
application of it had in no foregoing age been so frequent, nor the reception so general.   *Olympiodorus*, in
Photius's extracts, tells us of one *Libanius*, who practised this kind of military magic, and having promised
χωρὶς ὁπλιτῶν κατὰ βαρβάρων ἐνεργεῖν, *to perform
great things against the barbarians without soldiers*, was,
at the instances of the Emperess *Placidia*, put to Death,
when he was about to have given proofs of his abilities.
The Emperess shewed some kindness in her anger by
cutting him off at a time so convenient for his reputation.

But a more remarkable proof of the antiquity of
this notion may be found in St. *Chrysostom*'s book
de Sacerdotio, which exhibits a scene of enchantments
not exceeded by any romance of the middle age : he
supposes a spectator overlooking a field of battle
attended by one that points out all the various objects
of horror, the engines of destruction, and the arts of
slaughter.   Δεικνύτο δὲ ἔτι παρὰ τοῖς ἐναντίοις καὶ
πετομένους ἵππους διά τινος μαγγανείας, καὶ ὁπλίτας δι'
ἀέρος φερομένους, καὶ πάσην γοητείας δύναμιν καὶ ἰδέαν.
*Let him then proceed to show him in the opposite armies
horses flying by enchantment, armed men transported
through the air, and every power and form of magic.*
Whether St. *Chrysostom* believed that such performances were really to be seen in a day of battle, or only
endeavoured to enliven his description, by adopting
the notions of the vulgar, it is equally certain, that such
notions were in his time received, and that therefore
they were not imported from the *Saracens* in a later
age ; the wars with the *Saracens* however gave occasion
to their propagation, not only as bigotry naturally
discovers prodigies, but as the scene of action was
removed to a great distance.

The reformation did not immediately arrive at its meridian, and tho' day was gradually increasing upon us, the goblins of witchcraft still continued to hover in the twilight. In the time of Queen *Elizabeth* was the remarkable trial of the witches of *Warbois*, whose conviction is still commemorated in an annual sermon at *Huntingdon*. But in the reign of King *James*, in which this tragedy was written, many circumstances concurred to propagate and confirm this opinion. The King, who was much celebrated for his knowledge, had, before his arrival in *England*, not only examined in person a woman accused of witchcraft, but had given a very formal account of the practices and illusions of evil spirits, the compacts of witches, the ceremonies used by them, the manner of detecting them, and the justice of punishing them, in his Dialogues of *Dæmonologie*, written in the *Scottish* dialect, and published at *Edinburgh*. This book was, soon after his accession, reprinted at *London*, and as the ready way to gain King *James*'s favour was to flatter his speculations, the system of *Dæmonologie* was immediately adopted by all who desired either to gain preferment or not to lose it. Thus the doctrine of witchcraft was very powerfully inculcated; and as the greatest part of mankind have no other reason for their opinions than that they are in fashion, it cannot be doubted but this persuasion made a rapid progress, since vanity and credulity co-operated in its favour. The infection soon reached the parliament, who, in the first year of King *James*, made a law by which it was enacted, chap. xii. That " if any person shall use any invocation or con-juration of any evil or wicked spirit; 2. or shall consult, covenant with, entertain, employ, feed or reward any evil or cursed spirit to or for any intent or purpose; 3. or take up any dead man, woman or child out of the grave,--or the skin, bone, or any part of the dead person, to be employed or used in any manner of witchcraft, sorcery, charm, or enchantment; 4. or shall use, practise or exercise any sort of witchcraft, sorcery, charm, or enchantment; 5. whereby any person shall be destroyed, killed, wasted, consumed, pined, or lamed in any part of the body; 6. That every such person being convicted shall suffer death." This law was repealed in our own time.

Thus, in the time of *Shakespeare*, was the doctrine of witchcraft at once established by law and by the fashion, and it became not only unpolite, but criminal, to doubt it; and as prodigies are always seen in proportion as they are expected, witches were every day discovered, and multiplied so fast in some places, that bishop *Hall* mentions a village in *Lancashire*, where their number was greater than that of the houses. The jesuits and sectaries took advantage of this universal error, and endeavoured to promote the interest of their parties by pretended cures of persons afflicted by evil spirits; but they were detected and exposed by the clergy of the established church.

Upon this general infatuation *Shakespeare* might be easily allowed to found a play, especially since he has followed with great exactness such histories as were then thought true; nor can it be doubted that the scenes of enchantment, however they may now be ridiculed, were both by himself and his audience thought awful and affecting.

ACT I. SCENE x. (I. vii. 28 foll.)

The arguments by which Lady *Macbeth* persuades her husband to commit the murder, afford a proof of *Shakespeare*'s knowledge of human nature. She urges the excellence and dignity of courage, a glittering idea which has dazzled mankind from age to age, and animated sometimes the housebreaker, and sometimes the conqueror ; but this sophism *Macbeth* has for ever destroyed by distinguishing true from false fortitude, in a line and a half ; of which it may also be said, that they ought to bestow immortality on the author, though all his other productions had been lost.

> *I dare do all that may become a man,*
> *Who dares do more, is none.*

This topic, which has been always employed with too much success, is used in this scene with peculiar propriety, to a soldier by a woman. Courage is the distinguishing virtue of a soldier, and the reproach of cowardice cannot be borne by any man from a woman, without great impatience.

She then urges the oaths by which he had bound himself to murder *Duncan*, another art of sophistry by which men have sometimes deluded their consciences, and persuaded themselves that what would be criminal in others is virtuous in them ; this argument *Shakespeare*, whose plan obliged him to make *Macbeth* yield, has not confuted, though he might easily have shown that a former obligation could not be vacated by a latter : that obligations laid on us by a higher power, could not be overruled by obligations which we lay upon ourselves.

ACT II. SCENE ii. (II. i. 49-50.)

> *Now o'er one half the world*
> *Nature seems dead.*

That is, *over our hemisphere all action and motion seem to have ceased.* This image, which is perhaps the most striking that poetry can produce, has been adopted by *Dryden* in his *Conquest of* Mexico.

> *All things are hush'd as Nature's self lay dead,*
> *The mountains seem to nod their drowsy head ;*
> *The little birds in dreams their songs repeat,*
> *And sleeping flow'rs beneath the night dews sweat.*
> *Even lust and envy sleep !*

These lines, though so well known, I have transcribed,
that the contrast between them and this passage of
Shakespeare may be more accurately observed.

Night is described by two great poets, but one
describes a night of quiet, the other of perturbation.
In the night of *Dryden*, all the disturbers of the world
are laid asleep ; in that of *Shakespeare*, nothing but
sorcery, lust and murder, is awake. He that reads
Dryden, finds himself lull'd with serenity, and disposed to
solitude and contemplation. He that peruses *Shakespeare*,
looks round alarmed, and starts to find himself alone.
One is the night of a lover, the other, of a murderer.

ACT II. SCENE V. (II. iii. 118–21.)

> *Here, lay* Duncan ;
> *His silver skin laced with his golden blood,*
> *And his gash'd stabs look'd like a breach in nature*
> *For Ruin's wasteful entrance.*

Mr. *Pope* has endeavoured to improve one of these
lines by substituting *goary blood* for *golden blood* ; but
it may easily be admitted that he who could on such
an occasion talk of *lacing the silver skin*, would *lace it*
with *golden blood*. No amendment can be made to
this line, of which every word is equally faulty, but
by a general blot.

It is not improbable, that *Shakespeare* put these
forced and unnatural metaphors into the mouth of
Macbeth as a mark of artifice and dissimulation, to
show the difference between the studied language of
hypocrisy, and the natural outcries of sudden passion.
This whole speech so considered, is a remarkable
instance of judgment, as it consists entirely of antithesis and metaphor.

ACT III. SCENE ii. (III. i. 68–9.)

> *Mine eternal jewel*
> *Giv'n to the common enemy of man,*

It is always an entertainment to an inquisitive

reader, to trace a sentiment to its original source, and therefore though the term *enemy of man*, applied to the devil, is in itself natural and obvious, yet some may be pleased with being informed, that *Shakespeare* probably borrowed it from the first lines of the destruction of *Troy*, a book which he is known to have read.

That this remark may not appear too trivial, I shall take occasion from it to point out a beautiful passage of *Milton* evidently copied from a book of no greater authority, in describing the gates of hell. Book 2. v. 879. he says,

> ——— *On a sudden open fly,*
> *With impetuous recoil and jarring sound,*
> *Th' infernal doors, and on their hinges grate*
> *Harsh thunder.*

In the history of *Don Bellianis*, when one of the knights approaches, as I remember, the castle of *Brandezar*, the gates are said to open *grating harsh thunder upon their brazen hinges.*

Act IV. Scene i. (iv. i.)

As this is the chief scene of inchantment in the play, it is proper in this place to observe, with how much judgment *Shakespeare* has selected all the Circumstances of his infernal ceremonies, and how exactly he has conformed to common opinions and traditions.

Thrice the brinded cat hath mew'd.

The usual form in which familiar spirits are reported to converse with witches, is that of a cat. A witch, who was tried about half a century before the time of *Shakespeare*, had a cat named *Rutterkin*, as the spirit of one of those witches was *Grimalkin*; and when any mischief was to be done she used to bid *Rutterkin go and fly*, but once when she would have sent *Rutterkin* to torment a daughter of the countess of *Rutland*, instead of *going* or *flying*, he only cried *mew*, from whence she discovered that the lady was out of his power, the power of witches not being universal, but limited, as *Shakespeare* has taken care to inculcate.

> *Though his bark cannot be lost,*
> *Yet it shall be tempest tost.*

The common afflictions which the malice of witches produced were melancholy, fits, and loss of flesh, which are threatened by one of *Shakespeare*'s witches.

> *Weary sev'n-nights, nine times nine,*
> *Shall he dwindle, peak and pine.*

It was likewise their practice to destroy the cattle of their neighbours, and the farmers have to this day many ceremonies to secure their cows and other cattle from witchcraft ; but they seem to have been most suspected of malice against swine. *Shakespeare* has accordingly made one of his witches declare that she has been *killing swine*, and Dr. *Harsenet* observes, that about that time, *a sow could not be ill of the measles, nor a girl of the sullens, but some old woman was charged with witchcraft.*

> *Toad, that under the cold stone,*
> *Days and nights has, thirty-one,*
> *Swelter'd venom sleeping got ;*
> *Boil thou first i'th' charmed pot.*

Toads have likewise long lain under the reproach of being by some means accessary to witchcraft, for which reason *Shakespeare*, in the first scene of this play, calls one of the spirits *Padocke* or *Toad*, and now takes care to put a toad first into the pot. When *Vaninus* was seized at *Tholouse*, there was found at his lodgings *ingens*

Bufo Vitro inclusus, a great Toad shut in a Vial, upon
which those that prosecuted him *Veneficium exprobra-
bant, charged him,* I suppose, *with witchcraft.*

> *Fillet of a fenny snake,*
> *In the cauldron boil and bake ;*
> *Eye of newt, and toe of frog ;—*
> *For a charm,* &c.

The propriety of these ingredients may be known by
consulting the books *de Viribus Animalium* and *de
Mirabilibus Mundi,* ascribed to *Albertus Magnus,* in
which the reader, who has time and credulity, may
discover wonderful secrets.

> *Finger of birth-strangled babes,*
> *Ditch-deliver'd by a drab ;——*

It has been already mentioned in the law against
witches, that they are supposed to take up dead bodies
to use in enchantments, which was confessed by the
woman whom King *James* examined, and who had
of a dead body that was divided in one of their assem-
blies, two fingers for her share. It is observable that
Shakespeare, on this great occasion, which involves the
fate of a king, multiplies all the circumstances of
horror. The babe, whose finger is used, must be
strangled in its birth ; the grease must not only be
human, but must have dropped from a gibbet, the
gibbet of a murderer ; and even the sow, whose blood
is used, must have offended nature by devouring her
own farrow. These are touches of judgment and
genius.

> *And now about the cauldron sing——*
> *Black spirits and white,*
> *Blue spirits and grey,*
> *Mingle, mingle, mingle,*
> *You that mingle may.*

And in a former part,

>———*weyward sisters, hand in hand,*———
>*Thus do go about, about,*
>*Thrice to thine, and thrice to mine,*
>*And thrice again to make up nine!*

These two passages I have brought together, because they both seem subject to the objection of too much levity for the solemnity of enchantment, and may both be shown, by one quotation from *Camden*'s account of *Ireland*, to be founded upon a practice really observed by the uncivilised natives of that country. " When any one gets a fall, *says the informer of* Camden, he starts up, and *turning three times to the right* digs a hole in the earth; for they imagine that there is a spirit in the ground, and if he falls sick in two or three days, they send one of their women that is skilled in that way to the place, where she says, I call thee from the east, west, north and south, from the groves, the woods, the rivers, and the fens, from the *fairies red, black, white.*" There was likewise a book written before the time of *Shakespeare*, describing, amongst other properties, the *colours* of spirits.

Many other circumstances might be particularised, in which *Shakespeare* has shown his judgment and his knowledge.

Act V. Scene iii. (v. iii. 8.) English *Epicures.*

The reproach of epicurism, on which Mr. *Theobald* has bestowed a note, is nothing more than a natural invective uttered by an inhabitant of a barren country, against those who have more opportunities of luxury.

Act V. Scene viii. (v. vii. 77–9.)

>*Had I as many sons as I have hairs,*
>*I would not wish them to a fairer death.*
>*And so his knell is knoll'd.*

This incident is thus related from *Henry* of *Hunting-*

don by *Camden* in his *Remains*, from which the authour probably copied it.

When *Seyward*, the martial earl of *Northumberland*, understood that his son, whom he had sent in service against the *Scotchmen*, was slain, he demanded whether his wounds were in the fore part or hinder part of his body. When it was answered, in the fore part, he replied, " I am right glad ; neither wish I any other death to me or mine."

This play is deservedly celebrated for the propriety of its fictions, and solemnity, grandeur, and variety of its action ; but it has no nice discriminations of character, the events are too great to admit the influence of particular dispositions, and the course of the action necessarily determines the conduct of the agents.

The danger of ambition is well described ; and I know not whether it may not be said in defence of some parts which now seem improbable, that, in *Shakespeare*'s time, it was necessary to warn credulity against vain and illusive predictions.

The passions are directed to their true end. Lady *Macbeth* is merely detested ; and though the courage of *Macbeth* preserves some esteem, yet every reader rejoices at his fall.

CORIOLANUS.

Act III. Scene vi. (III. iii. 125 foll.)

> *Have the power still*
> *To banish your Defenders, 'till at length,*
> *Your ignorance, which finds not, 'till it feels, &c.*

Still retain the power of banishing your defenders, 'till your undiscerning folly, which can foresee no consequences, leave none in the city but yourselves, who are always labouring your own destruction.

It is remarkable, that, among the political maxims of the speculative *Harrington*, there is one which he might have borrowed from this speech. *The people*, says he, *cannot see, but they can feel.* It is not much to the honour of the people, that they have the same character of stupidity from their enemy and their friend. Such was the power of our authour's mind, that he looked through life in all its relations private and civil.

ACT IV. SCENE i. (IV. i. 7–9.)

> *Fortune's blows,*
> *When most struck home, being gentle, wounded, craves*
> *A noble cunning.*

The sense is, When fortune strikes her hardest blows, to be wounded, and yet continue calm, requires a generous policy. He calls this calmness *cunning*, because it is the effect of reflection and philosophy. Perhaps the first emotions of nature are nearly uniform, and one man differs from another in the power of endurance, as he is better regulated by precept and instruction.

> *They bore as heroes, but they felt as man.*

ACT IV. SCENE vi. (IV. vi. 99.) *The breath of garlick eaters.*

To smell of garlick was once such a brand of vulgarity, that garlick was a food forbidden to an ancient order of *Spanish* knights, mentioned by *Guevara.*

ACT IV. SCENE viii. (IV. vii. 51–3.)

> *And Power, unto itself most commendable,*
> *Hath not a tomb so evident, as a chair*
> *T'extol what it hath done.*

This is a common thought, but miserably ill expressed. The sense is, the virtue which delights to commend itself, will find the surest *Tomb* in that *Chair* wherein it holds forth its own commendations.

The Tragedy of *Coriolanus* is one of the most amusing of our authour's performances. The old man's merriment in *Menenius*; the lofty lady's dignity in *Volumnia*; the bridal modesty in *Virgilia*; the patrician and military haughtiness in *Coriolanus*; the plebeian malignity and tribunitian insolence in *Brutus* and *Sicinius*, make a very pleasing and interesting variety: and the various revolutions of the hero's fortune fill the mind with anxious curiosity. There is, perhaps too much bustle in the first act, and too little in the last.

JULIUS CAESAR

Of this tragedy many particular passages deserve regard, and the contention and reconcilement of *Brutus* and *Cassius* is universally celebrated; but I have never been strongly agitated in perusing it, and think it somewhat cold and unaffecting, compared with some other of *Shakespeare*'s plays; his adherence to the real story, and to *Roman* manners, seems to have impeded the natural vigour of his genius.

ANTONY AND CLEOPATRA.

Act III. Scene x. (iii. xi. 126-8.)

> *O that I were*
> *Upon the hill of Basan, to out-roar*
> *The borned herd.*

It is not without pity and indignation that the reader of this great Poet meets so often with this low jest, which is too much a favourite to be left out of either mirth or fury.

Act IV. Scene viii. (iv. ix. 15–16.)

> *Throw my heart*
> *Against the flint and hardness of my fault.*

The pathetick of *Shakespeare* too often ends in the ridiculous. It is painful to find the gloomy dignity of this noble scene destroyed by the intrusion of a conceit so far-fetched and unaffecting.

Act V. Scene v. (v. ii. 242.)   *The pretty worm of* Nilus.

Worm is the Teutonick word for *serpent* ; we have the *blind worm* and *slow worm* still in our language, and the *Norwegians* call an enormous monster, seen sometimes in the Northern ocean, the *Sea-worm*.

This Play keeps curiosity always busy, and the passions always interested. The continual hurry of the action, the variety of incidents, and the quick succession of one personage to another, call the mind forward without intermission from the first Act to the last. But the power of delighting is derived principally from the frequent changes of the scene ; for, except the feminine arts, some of which are too low, which distinguish *Cleopatra*, no character is very strongly discriminated. *Upton*, who did not easily miss what he desired to find, has discovered that the language of *Antony* is, with great skill and learning, made pompous and superb, according to his real practice. But I think his diction not distinguishable from that of others : the most tumid speech in the Play is that which *Cæsar* makes to *Octavia*.

The events, of which the principal are described according to history, are produced without any art of connection or care of disposition.

CYMBELINE.

ACT I. SCENE vii. (I. v. 18–24.)

> QUEEN.   *I will try the forces*
> *Of these thy compounds on such creatures as*
> *We count not worth the hanging, but none human, . .*
> CORNELIUS.   *Your Highness*
> *Shall from this practice but make hard your heart.*

There is in this passage nothing that much requires
a note, yet I cannot forbear to push it forward into
observation. The thought would probably have been
more amplified, had our authour lived to be shocked
with such experiments as have been published in later
times, by a race of men that have practised tortures
without pity, and related them without shame, and
are yet suffered to erect their heads among human
beings.

> *Cape saxa manu, cape robora, pastor.*

ACT II. SCENE iv. (II. iii. 118–20.)

> CLOTEN.   *The contract you pretend with that base wretch . . .*
> *. . . . . it is no contract, none.*

Here *Shakespeare* has not preserved, with his common
nicety, the uniformity of character. The speech of
Cloten is rough and harsh, but certainly not the talk
of one,

> *Who can't take two from twenty, for his heart,*
> *And leave eighteen.*

His argument is just and well enforced, and its preva-
lence is allowed throughout all civil nations : As for
rudeness, he seems not to be much undermatched.

ACT III. SCENE iii. (III. iii. 35–6.)

> ARVIRAGUS.   *What should we speak of*
> *When we are old as you ?*

This dread of an old age, unsupplied with matter

for discourse and meditation, is a sentiment natural and noble. No state can be more destitute than that of him who, when the delights of sense forsake him, has no pleasures of the mind.

ACT III. SCENE iii. (III. iii. 101.) *I stole these babes ;*

Shakespeare seems to intend *Belarius* for a good character, yet he makes him forget the injury which he has done to the young princes, whom he has robbed of a kingdom only to rob their father of heirs.

The latter part of this soliloquy is very inartificial, there being no particular reason why *Belarius* should now tell to himself what he could not know better by telling it.

ACT IV. SCENE iv. (IV. ii. 105–7.)
                    The snatches in his voice,
      And burst of speaking, were as his ; I'm absolute
      'Twas very Cloten.

This is one of our authour's strokes of observation. An abrupt and tumultuous utterance very frequently accompanies a confused and cloudy understanding.

ACT IV. SCENE v. (IV. ii. 258–81.)

For the obsequies of *Fidele*, a song was written by my unhappy friend, Mr. *William Collins* of *Chichester*, a man of uncommon learning and abilities. I shall give it a place at the end in honour of his memory.

ACT V. SCENE i. (V. i. 1 foll.)
            POSTHUMOUS. *Yea, bloody cloth,* &c.

This is a soliloquy of nature, uttered when the effervescence of a mind agitated and perturbed spontaneously and inadvertently discharges itself in words. The speech, throughout all its tenour, if the last conceit be excepted, seems to issue warm from the heart. He first condemns his own violence; then tries to disburden himself, by imputing part of the crime to *Pisanio*; he next sooths his mind to an artificial and momentary tranquillity, by trying to think that he has been only an instrument of the gods for the happiness of *Imogen*. He is now grown reasonable enough to determine, that having done so much evil he will do no more; that he will not fight against the country which he has already injured; but as life is not longer supportable, he will die in a just cause, and die with the obscurity of a man who does not think himself worthy to be remembered.

ACT V. SCENE iii. (v. iv. 26-8.)

> *Great Powers,*
> *If you will take this audit, take this life,*
> *And cancel those cold bonds.*

This equivocal use of *bonds* is another instance of our authour's infelicity in pathetick speeches.

This Play has many just sentiments, some natural dialogues, and some pleasing scenes, but they are obtained at the expence of much incongruity.

To remark the folly of the fiction, the absurdity of the conduct, the confusion of the names and manners of different times, and the impossibility of the events in any system of life, were to waste criticism upon unresisting imbecillity, upon faults too evident for detection, and too gross for aggravation.

TROILUS AND CRESSIDA.

ACT V. SCENE i. (v. i. 23.) *Cold palsies.*

This catalogue of loathsome maladies ends in the folio at *cold palsies*. This passage, as it stands, is in the quarto; the retrenchment was in my opinion judicious.

It may be remarked, though it proves nothing, that, of the few alterations made by *Milton* in the second edition of his wonderful poem, one was, an enlargement of the enumeration of diseases.

ACT V. SCENE vi. (v. iii. 23.)

CASSANDRA. *It is the purpose that makes strong the vow.*

The mad Prophetess speaks here with all the coolness and judgment of a skilful casuist. *The essence of a lawful vow, is a lawful purpose, and the vow of which the end is wrong must not be regarded as cogent.*

This Play is more correctly written than most of *Shakespeare's* compositions, but it is not one of those in which either the extent of his views or elevation of his fancy is fully displayed. As the story abounded with materials, he has exerted little invention; but he has diversified his characters with great variety, and preserved them with great exactness. His vicious characters sometimes disgust, but cannot corrupt, for both *Cressida* and *Pandarus* are detested and contemned. The comick characters seem to have been the favourites of the writer, they are of the superficial kind, and exhibit more of manners than nature, but they are copiously filled and powerfully impressed.

Shakespeare has in his story followed for the greater part the old book of *Caxton*, which was then very popular ; but the character of *Thersites*, of which it makes no mention, is a proof that this play was written after *Chapman* had published his version of *Homer*.

ROMEO AND JULIET.

Act I. Scene ii. (I. i. 181 foll.)
> *Why then, O brawling love! O loving hate!* &c.

Of these lines neither the sense nor occasion is very evident.   He is not yet in love with an enemy, and to love one and hate another is no such uncommon state, as can deserve all this toil of antithesis.

Act I. Scene iii. (I. ii. 25.)
> *Earth-treading stars that make dark* Heaven's *light.*

This nonsense should be reformed thus,
> *Earth-treading stars that make dark* even *light.*
>
> Warburton.

But why nonsense?   Is anything more commonly said, than that beauties eclipse the sun?   Has not *Pope* the thought and the word?

> *Sol through white curtains shot a tim'rous ray,*
> *And ope'd those eyes that must* eclipse the day.

Both the old and the new reading are philosophical nonsense, but they are both, and both equally poetical sense.

Act I. Scene iii. (I. ii. 26–8.)
> *Such comfort as do lusty young men feel,*
> *When well-apparel'd April on the heel*
> *Of limping Winter treads.*

To say, and to say in pompous words, that a *young man shall feel* as much in an assembly of beauties, *as young men feel in the month of April*, is surely to waste sound upon a very poor sentiment.   I read,
> *Such comfort as do lusty* yeomen *feel.*

You shall feel from the sight and conversation of these ladies, such hopes of happiness and such pleasure, as the farmer receives from the spring, when the plenty of the year begins, and the prospect of the harvest fills him with delight.

Act I. Scene iv. (i. iii. 92.)
That in gold clasps locks in the golden Story.

The *golden story* is perhaps the *golden legend*, a book in the darker ages of popery much read, and doubtless often exquisitely embellished, but of which *Canus*, one of the popish doctors, proclaims the author to have been *homo ferrei oris, plumbei cordis.*

Act I. Scene vi. (i. v. 34.)   *Good cousin* Capulet.

This cousin *Capulet* is *unkle* in the paper of invitation, but as *Capulet* is described as old, *cousin* is probably the right word in both places. I know not how *Capulet* and his lady might agree, their ages were very disproportionate ; he has been past masking for thirty years, and her age, as she tells Juliet, is but eight and twenty.

Act I. Chorus. (ii. Prologue.)

The use of this chorus is not easily discovered, it conduces nothing to the progress of the play, but relates what is already known, or what the next scenes will shew ; and relates it without adding the improvement of any moral sentiment.

Act II. Scene vi. (ii. vi. 15.)
Too swift arrives as tardy as too slow.

He that travels too fast is as long before he comes to the end of his journey, as he that travels slow. Precipitation produces mishap.

ACT III. SCENE i. (III. i. 2.)   *The day is hot.*

It is observed that in *Italy* almost all assassination are committed during the heat of summer.

ACT III. SCENE iii. (III. i. 183.)   *Affection makes him false.*

The charge of falshood on *Bentivolio*, though produced at hazard, is very just. The authour, who seems to intend the character of *Bentivolio* as good, meant perhaps to shew, how the best minds, in a state of faction and discord, are detorted to criminal partiality.

ACT III. SCENE viii. (III. v. 84.)
> *And, yet, no Man like he doth grieve my heart.*

Juliet's equivocations are rather too artful for a mind disturbed by the loss of a new lover.

ACT IV. SCENE ii. (IV. iii. 2–3.)
> *Leave me to myself to-night ;*
> *For I have need of many orisons.*

Juliet plays most of her pranks under the appearance of religion : perhaps *Shakespeare* meant to punish her hypocrisy.

ACT V. SCENE i. (V. i. 3.)
> *My bosom's Lord sits lightly on his throne,* &c.

These three lines are very gay and pleasing. But why does *Shakespeare* give *Romeo* this involuntary cheerfulness just before the extremity of unhappiness? Perhaps to shew the vanity of trusting to those uncertain and casual exaltations or depressions, which many consider as certain foretokens of good and evil.

ACT V. SCENE v. (V. iii. 229.)
> FRIAR.   *I will be brief.*

It is much to be lamented that the Poet did not

conclude the dialogue with the action, and avoid a narrative of events which the audience already knew.

This play is one of the most pleasing of our Author's performances. The scenes are busy and various, the incidents numerous and important, the catastrophe irresistibly affecting, and the process of the action carried on with such probability, at least with such congruity to popular opinions, as tragedy requires.

Here is one of the few attempts of *Shakespeare* to exhibit the conversation of gentlemen, to represent the airy sprightliness of juvenile elegance. Mr. *Dryden* mentions a tradition, which might easily reach his time, of a declaration made by *Shakespeare,* that *he was obliged to kill* Mercutio *in the third act, lest he should have been killed by him.* Yet he thinks him *no such formidable person, but that he might have lived through the play, and died in his bed,* without danger to a poet. *Dryden* well knew, had he been in quest of truth, that, in a pointed sentence, more regard is commonly had to the words than the thought, and that it is very seldom to be rigorously understood. *Mercutio's* wit, gaiety and courage, will always procure him friends that wish him a longer life; but his death is not precipitated, he has lived out the time allotted him in the construction of the play; nor do I doubt the ability of *Shakespeare* to have continued his existence, though some of his sallies are perhaps out of the reach of *Dryden;* whose genius was not very fertile of merriment, nor ductile to humour, but acute, argumentative, comprehensive, and sublime.

The Nurse is one of the characters in which the Authour delighted: he has, with great subtilty of distinction, drawn her at once loquacious and secret, obsequious and insolent, trusty and dishonest.

His comick scenes are happily wrought, but his

pathetick strains are always polluted with some unexpected depravations. His persons, however distressed, *have a conceit left them in their misery, a miserable conceit.*

HAMLET.

ACT I. SCENE i.   (I. i. 63.)
He smote the sleaded Polack *on the ice.*

Polack was, in that age, the term for an inhabitant of *Poland* : *Polaque,* French. As in a translation of *Passeratius*'s epitaph on *Henry* III. of *France,* published by *Camden* :

Whether thy chance or choice thee hither brings,
Stay, passenger, and wail the best of kings.
This little stone a great king's heart doth hold,
Who rul'd the fickle French and Polacks *bold :*
So frail are even the highest earthly things.
Go, passenger, and wail the hap of kings.

ACT I. SCENE i.   (I. i. 128.)   *If thou hast any sound.*

The speech of *Horatio* to the spectre is very elegant and noble, and congruous to the common traditions of the causes of apparitions.

ACT I. SCENE i.   (I. i. 153 foll.)   *Whether in sea or fire, &c.*

According to the pneumatology of that time, every element was inhabited by its peculiar order of spirits, who had dispositions different, according to their various places of abode. The meaning therefore is, that all *spirits extravagant,* wandering out of their element, whether aerial spirits visiting earth, or earthly spirits ranging the air, return to their station, to their proper limits in which they are *confined.*

Act I. Scene ix. (I. v. 154.) *Swear by my sword.*

Mr. *Garrick* produced me a passage, I think, in *Brantôme*, from which it appeared, that it was common to swear upon the sword, that is, upon the cross which the old swords had upon the hilt.

Act II. Scene ii. (II. i. 114–17.)

> *It is as proper to our age*
> *To cast beyond ourselves in our opinions,*
> *As it is common for the younger sort*
> *To lack discretion.*

This is not the remark of a weak man. The vice of age is too much suspicion. Men long accustomed to the wiles of life *cast* commonly *beyond themselves*, let their cunning go further than reason can attend it. This is always the fault of a little mind, made artful by long commerce with the world.

Act II. Scene iv. (II. ii.)

Polonius is a man bred in courts, exercised in business, stored with observation, confident of his knowledge, proud of his eloquence, and declining into dotage. His mode of oratory is truly represented as designed to ridicule the practice of those times, of prefaces that made no introduction, and of method that embarrassed rather than explained. This part of his character is accidental, the rest is natural. Such a man is positive and confident, because he knows that his mind was once strong, and knows not that it is become weak. Such a man excels in general principles, but fails in the particular application. He is knowing in retrospect, and ignorant in foresight. While he depends upon his memory, and can draw from his repositories of knowledge, he utters weighty sentences, and gives useful counsel ; but as the mind in its enfeebled state cannot be kept long busy and intent, the old man is subject to

sudden dereliction of his faculties, he loses the order
of his ideas, and entangles himself in his own thoughts,
till he recovers the leading principle, and falls again
into his former train. This idea of dotage encroaching
upon wisdom, will solve all the phænomena of the
character of *Polonius*.

ACT II. SCENE vi. (II. ii. 269.) *The shadow of a dream.*

Shakespeare has accidentally inverted an expression
of *Pindar*, that the state of humanity is σκιᾶς ὄναρ,
the *dream* of a *shadow*.

ACT III. SCENE ii. (III. i. 56 foll.) *To be, or not to be?*

Of this celebrated soliloquy, which bursting from
a man distracted with contrariety of desires, and over-
whelmed with the magnitude of his own purposes, is
connected rather in the speaker's mind, than on his
tongue, I shall endeavour to discover the train, and
to shew how one sentiment produces another.

Hamlet, knowing himself injured in the most enormous and atrocious degree, and seeing no means of
redress, but such as must expose him to the extremity of
hazard, meditates on his situation in this manner:
*Before I can form any rational scheme of action under
this pressure of distress*, it is necessary to decide, whether,
after our present state, we are to be or not to be. That
is the question, which, as it shall be answered, will
determine, *whether 'tis nobler*, and more suitable to the
dignity of reason, *to suffer the outrages of fortune* patiently,
or to take arms against *them*, and by opposing end them,
though perhaps with the loss of life. If *to die*, were *to
sleep, no more, and by a sleep to end* the miseries of our
nature, such a sleep were *devoutly to be wished*; but
if *to sleep* in death, be *to dream*, to retain our powers of
sensibility, we must *pause* to consider, *in that sleep of
death what dreams may come*. This consideration

makes calamity so long endured ; *for who would bear*
the vexations of life, which might be ended *by a bare*
bodkin, but that he is afraid of something in unknown
futurity? This fear it is that gives efficacy to conscience, which, by turning the mind upon *this regard*,
chills the ardour of *resolution*, checks the vigour of
enterprise, and makes the *current* of desire stagnate in
inactivity.

We may suppose that he would have applied these
general observations to his own case, but that he
discovered *Ophelia*.

ACT III. SCENE ii. (III. i. 70.) *The whips and scorns of time.*

It may be remarked, that *Hamlet*, in his enumeration
of miseries, forgets, whether properly or not, that he
is a prince, and mentions many evils to which inferior
stations only are exposed.

ACT III. SCENE II. (III. i. 89).   *Nymph, in thy orisons, &c.*

This is a touch of nature. *Hamlet*, at the sight of
Ophelia, does not immediately recollect, that he is
to personate madness, but makes her an address grave
and solemn, such as the foregoing meditation excited
in his thoughts.

ACT III. SCENE v.

I know not why our editors should, with such
implacable anger, persecute our predecessors. Οἱ
νεκροὶ μὴ δάκνουσιν the dead it is true can make no
resistance, they may be attacked with great security ;
but since they can neither feel nor mend, the safety
of mauling them seems greater than the pleasure ;
nor perhaps would it much misbeseem us to remember,
amidst our triumphs over the *nonsensical* and the *sense-*
less, that we likewise are men ; that *debemur morti*,
and as *Swift* observed to *Burnet*, shall soon be among the
dead ourselves.

Act III. Scene ix. (III. iii. 94–5.)

> *That his soul may be as damn'd and black*
> *As hell, whereto it goes.*

This speech, in which *Hamlet*, represented as a virtuous character, is not content with taking blood for blood, but contrives damnation for the man that he would punish, is too horrible to be read or to be uttered.

Act IV. Scene v. (IV. v. 84.)   *In bugger mugger to interr him.*

All the modern editions that I have consulted give it,

> *In* private *to inter him* ;——

That the words now replaced are better, I do not undertake to prove ; it is sufficient that they are *Shakespeare*'s : If phraseology is to be changed as words grow uncouth by disuse, or gross by vulgarity, the history of every language will be lost ; we shall no longer have the words of any authour ; and, as these alterations will be often unskilfully made, we shall in time have very little of his meaning.

Act IV. Scene ix. (IV. vii. 20–1.)

> *Would, like the spring that turneth wood to stone,*
> *Convert his gyves to graces.*

This simile is neither very seasonable in the deep interest of this conversation, nor very accurately applied. If the *spring* had changed base metals to gold, the thought had been more proper.

Act V. Scene i. (V. i. 84–5.)

> *This might be the pate of a politician, which this ass o'er-offices.*

In the quarto, for *over-offices* is, *over-reaches*, which agrees better with the sentence. I believe both the words were *Shakespeare*'s. An authour in revising his work, when his original ideas have faded from his

NOTES   o

mind, and new observations have produced new sentiments, easily introduces images which have been more newly impressed upon him, without observing their want of congruity to the general texture of his original design.

Act V. Scene ii. (v. i. 254.)

> *Allow'd her virgin* RITES.

The old quarto reads virgin CRANTS.

I have been informed by an anonymous correspondent, that *crants* is the *German* word for *garlands*, and I suppose it was retained by us from the *Saxons*. To carry *garlands* before the bier of a maiden, and to hang them over her grave, is still the practice in rural parishes.

Crants therefore was the original word, which the authour, discovering it to be provincial, and perhaps not understood, changed to a term more intelligible, but less proper. *Maiden rites* give no certain or definite image. He might have put *maiden wreaths*, or *maiden garlands*, but he perhaps bestowed no thought upon it, and neither genius nor practice will always supply a hasty writer with the most proper diction.

Act V. Scene iii. (v. ii. 6–7.)

> *Rashly,*
> *And prais'd be rashness for it.*

Hamlet, delivering an account of his escape, begins with saying, That he *rashly*——and then is carried into a reflection upon the weakness of human wisdom. I rashly——praised be rashness for it—*Let us* not think these events casual, but *let us know*, that is, *take notice and remember*, that we sometimes succeed by *indiscretion*, when we *fail* by *deep plots*, and infer the perpetual superintendence and *agency* of the *Divinity*. The observation is just, and will be allowed by every human being who shall reflect on the course of his own life.

ACT V. SCENE iii. (v. ii. 41-2.)

> *As Peace should still her wheaten garland wear,*
> *And stand a COMMA 'tween their amities ;*

The expression of our authour is, like many of his phrases, sufficiently constrained and affected, but it is not incapable of explanation. The *Comma* is the note of *connection* and continuity of sentences ; the *Period* is the note of *abruption* and disjunction. *Shakespeare* had it perhaps in his mind to write, That unless *England* complied with the mandate, *war should put a period to their amity* ; he altered his mode of diction, and thought that, in an opposite sense, he might put, That *Peace should stand a* Comma *between their amities*. This is not an easy style ; but is it not the style of *Shakespeare ?*

ACT V. SCENE v. (v. ii. 240.)

HAMLET. *Give me your pardon, Sir. I've done you wrong.*

I wish *Hamlet* had made some other defence ; it is unsuitable to the character of a good or a brave man, to shelter himself in falsehood.

If the dramas of *Shakespeare* were to be characterised, each by the particular excellence which distinguishes it from the rest, we must allow to the tragedy of *Hamlet* the praise of variety. The incidents are so numerous, that the argument of the play would make a long tale. The scenes are interchangeably diversified with merriment and solemnity ; with merriment that includes judicious and instructive observations, and solemnity, not strained by poetical violence above the natural sentiments of man. New characters appear from time to time in continual succession, exhibiting various forms of life and particular modes of conversation. The pretended madness of *Hamlet* causes much mirth, the mournful distraction of *Ophelia* fills the heart with tenderness, and every personage produces the effect intended, from the apparition that in the first act chills the blood with horror, to the fop in the last, that exposes affectation to just contempt.

The conduct is perhaps not wholly secure against objections. The action is indeed for the most part in continual progression, but there are some scenes which neither forward nor retard it. Of the feigned madness of *Hamlet* there appears no adequate cause, for he does nothing which he might not have done with the reputation of sanity. He plays the madman most, when he treats *Ophelia* with so much rudeness, which seems to be useless and wanton cruelty.

Hamlet is, through the whole play, rather an instrument than an agent. After he has, by the stratagem of the play, convicted the King, he makes no attempt to punish him, and his death is at last effected by an incident which *Hamlet* has no part in producing.

The catastrophe is not very happily produced; the exchange of weapons is rather an expedient of necessity, than a stroke of art. A scheme might easily have been formed, to kill *Hamlet* with the dagger, and *Laertes* with the bowl.

The poet is accused of having shewn little regard to poetical justice, and may be charged with equal neglect of poetical probability. The apparition left the regions of the dead to little purpose; the revenge which he demands is not obtained but by the death of him that was required to take it; and the gratification which would arise from the destruction of an usurper and a murderer, is abated by the untimely death of *Ophelia*, the young, the beautiful, the harmless, and the pious.

OTHELLO.

ACT I. SCENE viii. (I. iii. 134 foll.)
> *I spoke of most disastrous chances,*
> *Of moving accidents by flood and field;*

Whoever ridicules this account of the progress of love, shews his ignorance, not only of history, but of nature and manners. It is no wonder that, in any age, or in any nation, a lady, recluse, timorous, and delicate, should desire to hear of events and scenes which she could never see, and should admire the man who had endured dangers, and performed actions, which, however great, were yet magnified by her timidity.

ACT II. SCENE viii. (II. i. 308–9.)
> *The thought whereof*
> *Doth, like a poisonous mineral, gnaw my inwards.*

This is philosophical. Mineral poisons kill by corrosion.

ACT III. SCENE v. (III. iii. 90.) *Excellent Wretch!*

The meaning of the word *wretch*, is not generally understood. It is now, in some parts of *England*, a term of the softest and fondest tenderness. It expresses the utmost degree of amiableness, joined with an idea, which perhaps all tenderness includes, of feebleness, softness, and want of protection. *Othello*, considering *Desdemona* as excelling in beauty and virtue, soft and timorous by her sex, and by her situation absolutely in his power, calls her, *Excellent Wretch*. It may be expressed,

> *Dear, harmless, helpless Excellence.*

Act III. **Scene** v. (III. iii. 206.)

> *She did deceive her father, marrying you.*

This and the following argument of *Iago* ought to be deeply impressed on every reader. Deceit and falsehood, whatever conveniences they may for a time promise or produce, are, in the sum of life, obstacles to happiness. Those who profit by the cheat, distrust the deceiver, and the act by which kindness was sought, puts an end to confidence.

The same objection may be made with a lower degree of strength against the imprudent generosity of disproportionate marriages. When the first heat of passion is over, it is easily succeeded by suspicion, that the same violence of inclination which caused one irregularity, may stimulate to another; and those who have shewn, that their passions are too powerful for their prudence, will, with very slight appearances against them, be censured, as not very likely to restrain them by their virtue.

Act III. **Scene** vi. (III. iii. 262–3.)

> *Let her down the wind*
> *To prey at fortune.*

The falconers always let fly the hawk against the wind; if she flies with the wind behind her, she seldom returns. If therefore a hawk was for any reason to be dismissed, she was *let down the wind*, and from that time shifted for herself, and *prey'd at fortune*. This was told me by the late Mr. *Clark*.

Act III. **Scene** xi. (III. iv. 102.)

> *'Tis not a year, or two, shews us a man.*

From this line it may be conjectured, that the authour intended the action of this play to be considered as longer than is marked by any note of time. Since their arrival at *Cyprus*, to which they were hurried on their wedding-night, the fable seems to have been in one continual progress, nor can I see any vacuity into which a *year or two*, or even a month or two, could be put.   On the night of *Othello*'s arrival, a feast was proclaimed ; at that feast *Cassio* was degraded, and immediately applies to *Desdemona* to get him restored.   *Iago* indeed advises *Othello* to hold him off a while, but there is no reason to think, that he has been held off long.   A little longer interval would increase the probability of the story, though it might violate the rules of the drama.

Act IV. Scene i. (iv. i. 40–2.)
Nature would not invest herself in such shadowing passion without some instruction.

There has always prevailed in the world an opinion, that when any great calamity happens at a distance, notice is given of it to the sufferer by some dejection or perturbation of mind, of which he discovers no external cause.   This is ascribed to that general communication of one part of the universe with another, which is called sympathy and antipathy ; or to the secret monition, *instruction*, and influence of a superior Being, which superintends the order of Nature and of life.   *Othello* says, *Nature could not invest herself in such shadowing passion, without* instruction.   *It is not words that shakes me thus.*   This passion which spreads its clouds over me is the effect of some agency more than the operation of words ; it is one of those notices which men have of unseen calamities.

Act V. Scene vi. (v. ii. 21–2.)
This Sorrow's heavenly ;
It strikes, where it doth love.

I wish these two lines could be honestly ejected.   It is the fate of *Shakespeare* to counteract his own pathos.

Act V. Scene vi. (v. ii. 63-5.)

> *Oh perjur'd woman ! thou dost stone my heart,*
> *And mak'st me call, what I intend to do,*
> *A murder, which I thought a sacrifice.*

This line is difficult. *Thou hast hardened my heart, and makest me* kill thee with the rage of a *murderer,* when *I thought to have sacrificed* thee to justice with the calmness of a priest striking a victim.

It must not be omitted, that one of the elder quarto's reads, *thou dost stone thy heart* ; which I suspect to be genuine. The meaning then will be, *thou forcest me* to dismiss thee from the world in the state of the *murdered* without preparation for death, *when I intended* that thy punishment should have been *a sacrifice* atoning for thy crime.

I am glad that I have ended my revisal of this dreadful scene. It is not to be endured.

The beauties of this play impress themselves so strongly upon the attention of the reader, that they can draw no aid from critical illustration. The fiery openness of *Othello,* magnanimous, artless, and credulous, boundless in his confidence, ardent in his affection, inflexible in his resolution, and obdurate in his revenge ; the cool malignity of *Iago,* silent in his resentment, subtle in his designs, and studious at once of his interest and his vengeance ; the soft simplicity of *Desdemona,* confident of merit, and conscious of innocence, her artless perseverance in her suit, and her slowness to suspect that she can be suspected, are such proofs of *Shakespeare's* skill in human nature, as, I suppose, it is vain to seek in any modern writer. The gradual progress which *Iago* makes in the Moor's conviction, and the circumstances which he employs to inflame him, are so artfully natural, that, though it will perhaps not be said of him as he says of himself, that he is *a man not easily jealous*, yet we cannot but pity him when at last we find him *perplexed in the extreme.*

There is always danger lest wickedness conjoined with abilities should steal upon esteem, though it misses of approbation ; but the character of *Iago* is so conducted, that he is from the first scene to the last hated and despised.

Even the inferiour characters of this play would be very conspicuous in any other piece, not only for their justness but their strength. *Cassio* is brave, benevolent, and honest, ruined only by his want of stubbornness to resist an insidious invitation. *Roderigo*'s suspicious credulity, and impatient submission to the cheats which he sees practised upon him, and which by persuasion he suffers to be repeated, exhibit a strong picture of a weak mind betrayed by unlawful desires, to a false friend ; and the virtue of *Æmilia* is such as we often find, worn loosely, but not cast off, easy to commit small crimes, but quickened and alarmed at atrocious villanies.

The Scenes from the beginning to the end are busy, varied by happy interchanges, and regularly promoting the progression of the story ; and the narrative in the end, though it tells but what is known already, yet is necessary to produce the death of *Othello*.

Had the scene opened in *Cyprus*, and the preceding incidents been occasionally related, there had been little wanting to a drama of the most exact and scrupulous regularity.

MACBETH.

(*The Rambler*, No. 168.)

———— *Decipit*
Frons prima multos, rara mens intelligit
Quod interiore condidit cura angulo. PHÆDRUS.

The tinsel glitter, and the specious mien,
Delude the most ; few pry behind the scene.

IT has been observed by *Boileau*, that "a mean or common thought expressed in pompous diction, generally pleases more than a new or noble sentiment delivered in low and vulgar language ; because the number is greater of those whom custom has enabled to judge of words, than whom study has qualified to examine things."

This solution might satisfy, if such only were offended with meanness of expression as are unable to distinguish propriety of thought, and to separate propositions or images from the vehicles by which they are conveyed to the understanding. But this kind of disgust is by no means confined to the ignorant or superficial ; it operates uniformly and universally upon readers of all classes ; every man, however profound or abstracted, perceives himself irresistibly alienated by low terms ; they who profess the most zealous adherence to truth are forced to admit that she owes part of her charms to her ornaments ; and loses much of her power over the soul, when she appears disgraced by a dress uncouth or ill adjusted.

We are all offended by low terms, but are not disgusted alike by the same compositions, because we do not all agree to censure the same terms as low. No word is naturally or intrinsically meaner than another ;

our opinion therefore of words, as of other things arbitrarily and capriciously established, depends wholly upon accident and custom.   The cottager thinks those apartments splendid and spacious, which an inhabitant of palaces will despise for their inelegance ; and to him who has passed most of his hours with the delicate and polite, many expressions will seem sordid, which another, equally acute, may hear without offence ; but a mean term never fails to displease him to whom it appears mean, as poverty is certainly and invariably despised, though he who is poor in the eyes of some, may, by others, be envied for his wealth.

Words become low by the occasions to which they are applied, or the general character of them who use them ; and the disgust which they produce, arises from the revival of those images with which they are commonly united.   Thus if, in the most solemn discourse, a phrase happens to occur which has been successfully employed in some ludicrous narrative, the gravest auditor finds it difficult to refrain from laughter, when they who are not prepossessed by the same accidental association, are utterly unable to guess the reason of his merriment.   Words which convey ideas of dignity in one age, are banished from elegant writing or conversation in another, because they are in time debased by vulgar mouths, and can be no longer heard without the involuntary recollection of unpleasing images.

When *Macbeth* is confirming himself in the horrid purpose of stabbing his king, he breaks out amidst his emotions into a wish natural to a murderer :

    —— Come, thick night !
And pall thee in the dunnest smoke of hell,
That my keen knife see not the wound it makes ;
Nor heav'n peep through the blanket of the dark,
To cry, Hold ! hold !

In this passage is exerted all the force of poetry, that force which calls new powers into being, which embodies sentiment, and animates matter ; yet, perhaps, scarce any man now peruses it without some disturbance of his attention from the counteraction of the words to the ideas.   What can be more dreadful than to implore the presence of night, invested, not in common obscurity, but in the smoke of hell?   Yet the efficacy of this invocation is destroyed by the insertion of an epithet now seldom heard but in the stable, and *dun* night may come or go without any other notice than contempt.

If we start into raptures when some hero of the Iliad tells us that δόρυ μαίνεται, his lance rages with eagerness to destroy ; if we are alarmed at the terrour of the soldiers commanded by *Cæsar* to hew down the sacred grove, who dreaded, says *Lucan*, lest the axe aimed at the oak should fly back upon the striker :

—— *Si robora sacra ferirent,*
In sua credebant redituras membra secures,

None dares with impious steel the grove to rend,
Lest on himself the destin'd stroke descend ;

we cannot surely but sympathise with the horrours of a wretch about to murder his master, his friend, his benefactor, who suspects that the weapon will refuse its office, and start back from the breast which he is preparing to violate.   Yet this sentiment is weakened by the name of an instrument used by butchers and cooks in the meanest employments : we do not immediately conceive that any crime of importance is to be committed with a *knife* ; or who does not, at last, from the long habit of connecting a knife with sordid offices, feel aversion rather than terrour?

Macbeth proceeds to wish, in the madness of guilt, that the inspection of heaven may be intercepted,

and that he may, in the involutions of infernal darkness, escape the eye of Providence. This is the utmost
extravagance of determined wickedness; yet this is so
debased by two unfortunate words, that while I endeavour to impress on my reader the energy of the
sentiment, I can scarce check my risibility, when the
expression forces itself upon my mind; for who,
without some relaxation of his gravity, can hear of the
avengers of guilt *peeping through a blanket?*

These imperfections of diction are less obvious to
the reader, as he is less acquainted with common
usages; they are therefore wholly imperceptible to
a foreigner, who learns our language from books, and
will strike a solitary academick less forcibly than
a modish lady.

Among the numerous requisites that must concur to
complete an author, few are of more importance than
an early entrance into the living world. The seeds
of knowledge may be planted in solitude, but must be
cultivated in publick. Argumentation may be taught
in colleges, and theories formed in retirement; but
the artifice of embellishment, and the powers of
attraction, can be gained only by general converse.

An acquaintance with prevailing customs and
fashionable elegance is necessary likewise for other
purposes. The injury that grand imagery suffers
from unsuitable language, personal merit may fear from
rudeness and indelicacy. When the success of *Æneas*
depended on the favour of the queen upon whose
coasts he was driven, his celestial protectress thought
him not sufficiently secured against rejection by his
piety or bravery, but decorated him for the interview
with preternatural beauty. Whoever desires, for his
writings or himself, what none can reasonably con-
temn, the favour of mankind, must add grace to
strength, and make his thoughts agreeable as well as

useful. Many complain of neglect who never tried to attract regard. It cannot be expected that the patrons of science or virtue should be solicitous to discover excellencies, which they who possess them shade and disguise. Few have abilities so much needed by the rest of the world as to be caressed on their own terms ; and he that will not condescend to recommend himself by external embellishments, must submit to the fate of just sentiment meanly expressed, and be ridiculed and forgotten before he is understood.

NOTE

PAGE vii. The *Proposals* of 1745 are not lost. Some half-dozen copies are now known of *Miscellaneous Observations on the Tragedy of Macbeth*, in which the single folio leaf of *Proposals for a New Edition of Shakespear* has survived. These Proposals are, however, a mere advertisement, with a specimen of the types which it was intended to use.

The project was abandoned for a sufficient reason. Jacob Tonson, the publisher, claimed copyright in Shakespeare's works, and threatened Cave with legal proceedings. See Courtney, *Bibliography of Johnson*, pp. 17–18.

The *Proposals* of 1756 were until recently known only from reprints in the *London Chronicle* (1757) and in collected editions of Johnson's works. See Courtney, *op. cit.* p. 78. But a copy of the original was discovered in 1923, and has been reprinted (Oxford, 1923); it enables us to correct certain misprints.

It is now known that there were two distinct impressions of Johnson's edition of Shakespeare in 1765. This was first pointed out by Mr. H. F. B. Brett-Smith (*Times Literary Supplement*, 15 May 1919), who called attention to variations in the setting and arrangement of the Prefaces. It is clear that not only the first volume, but the whole eight volumes, were reset (as indeed was stated at the time; see Courtney, p. 107).

This selection was set up from Sir Walter Raleigh's own copy, which was of the first impression, and certain errors were reproduced which have now been corrected by reference to the second impression or to the later editions produced by George Steevens.

Mr. David Nichol Smith points out that in the Preface (p. 23, line 9 from foot) a new sentence was introduced in the edition of 1778—the second, that is, of the *Plays* by Johnson-Steevens in ten **volumes**. The new sentence, which follows the words *crosses of love*, is characteristic : *What he does best, he soon ceases to do.* This is interesting as a proof that Johnson had more to do with the later editions than is commonly supposed, and as an example of what he could do with words of one syllable.

PAGE 136, l. 4. This confused statement is in the edition of 1778 amended as follows :

The second and third parts of *Henry* VI. were printed in 1600. When *Henry* V. was written, we know not, but it was printed likewise in 1600, and therefore before the publication of the first part : the first part of *Henry* VI. had been often *shewn on the stage*, and would certainly have appeared in its place had the author been the publisher.

PAGE 148. Dr. Henry Bradley supplied the reference to Celsus, viii. 4 : A suturis se deceptum esse Hippocrates memoriae prodidit, more scilicet magnorum virorum, et fiduciam magnorum rerum habentium. Nam levia ingenia, quia nihil habent, nihil sibi detrahunt : magno ingenio, multaque nihilominus habituro, convenit etiam simplex veri erroris confessio.

R. W. C.

January 1925.

PRINTED IN GREAT BRITAIN
AT THE UNIVERSITY PRESS, OXFORD
BY CHARLES BATEY, PRINTER TO THE UNIVERSITY